Pottery: Materials and Techniques

by the same author

★

UNDERSTANDING POTTERY GLAZES

Glaze experiments by students working on similar lines to those suggested in chapter 7 (see page 11 for full description)

Pottery:
Materials and Techniques

DAVID GREEN

FABER AND FABER LIMITED
24 Russell Square, London

First published in mcmlxvii
by Faber and Faber Limited
24 Russell Square, London, W.C.1
Printed in Great Britain
by Ebenezer Baylis and Son Limited
The Trinity Press, Worcester, and London

© *1967 by David Green*

To the memory of
Bill and Rhoda Lambshead

Acknowledgements

I am grateful to the Principal, Mr. A. G. Tennant Moon, and my colleagues at Carlisle College of Art and Design for their help and encouragement during the production of this book. In particular mention should be made of the excellent photographs – more than half the total number – produced for me by Mr. Geoffrey Sheard; the continuous assistance given by Mr. David Graham, my colleague in the Ceramic Department; the constant supply of reference material provided by the librarians, Mr. Raymund Fitzsimons and Mrs. M. K. Davidson; the constructive criticism of Mr. Roy Barker and the typing done by Mrs. McIntyre.

I should also like to thank Mr. Peter Browning for his help with the bibliography to Chapter 1; T.R.H. for his criticism of the early proofs; Mr. William Ruscoe for the original plans from which the down-draught kiln discussed in Chapter 5 was evolved and Mr. A. E. Dodd, Information Officer of the British Ceramic Research Association, for his corrections in Chapter 3.

Those firms which have provided photographs are noted in the List of Plates, and I am indebted for their willingness to supply them. Many of the other photographs are of the work of students or children, and this affords me the opportunity not only to thank them for the loan of their work, but also to say how much I have enjoyed working with them. Their enthusiasm, together with that of many others whose work it was not possible to illustrate, has been a constant source of inspiration.

Further I should like to thank Miss Rosemary Goad and Mr. Michael Wright of Faber and Faber Ltd. for the care they have taken over the production of this book.

Contents

The Plates

Drawings in the Text

(Drawings by the author)

List of Tables in the Text

Foreword

My aim in this book is to help anyone who is enthusiastic to do some pottery, or who would like to introduce this craft to the children they teach, by firstly providing guidance on the choice of materials and equipment from those available on the market. Secondly I aim to give enough information on techniques – apart from the elaborate art of throwing – to enable newcomers to start, and to provide, through annotated bibliographies, information about the recognized manuals covering aspects of the craft in detail. Thirdly I have attempted to outline the whole field of ceramics, including the geology and chemistry of the materials and the history of their use in technology as well as the domestic field.

Good clay vessels are pleasing to use and there is an added joy associated with the products of the skilled hand craftsman. In recent turbulent years the number of craftsman potters all over the world has increased sharply, and facilities for the craft have been made available in schools or colleges of all kinds. This is not merely the result of fashion; clay is an appealing substance which casts a spell on children and adults alike. Clay responds more readily than most materials to the hand and the mind; it mirrors exactly the co-ordination between them and there is no other which can yield such a wealth of texture, form and colour. It can be used expressively with little practice and without the aid of tools, even though for industrial application it demands exceptional skill allied to generations of accumulated technical knowledge.

There are few other crafts for which raw materials are so readily accessible, and there is no other craft about which scientific and historical study can reveal more about the nature of the Earth or the evolution of our environment. As this background of ceramics can be studied along with intensely exciting creative work it has the power to breathe life into the hazy scientific knowledge of most artists, and, as there is also a strong fine art side to ceramics, I feel that they have much to offer towards a liberal education. Part Two of this book has been written with this exchange of knowledge between arts and science students in schools very much in mind though the study holds a fascination for so many of us.

The three parts of the book are independent of one another so that a reader seeking first of all information about tools, materials or techniques will find it collected together in Part Three. Part One is addressed especially to teachers or anyone else who is faced with the mixture of children and clay. The value of art and craftwork is now so well understood that this section is only included to emphasize certain points and to introduce the important books listed in the bibliography on Teaching to which all those connected with art or craftwork are heavily indebted. Without the persistent efforts of their authors, as well as some whose books on pottery are listed at the ends of other chapters, we should still be doing pioneering work today.

PART ONE

A small but impressive version of the famous T'ang horse models which have survived in some numbers because they were placed in tombs. Some of the models are over 30 inches high; they are hollow, earthenware, and generally lead glazed

Chapter 1

Teaching With Clay

Recent changes in the pattern of education are nowhere more marked than in art. The subject has come rapidly to the fore in primary and secondary schools and there is now general agreement on its importance in higher education and industry.

There are several reasons for the stress on art or craftwork in schools which each of us will define in our own ways. Here are some suggestions:

1. It has been realized that creativity is a basic ingredient of our make-up, and without its fulfilment we cannot grow as balanced, well-adjusted people. For adults the daily routine may offer fulfilment in a variety of ways, not all of which are connected with art. For instance, planning a business or cultivating a garden are occupations of a kind that can exercise the creative side of a man in much the same way as painting or any other art form. Not many such activities can, however, be practised by children, whose creativity can only be satisfied by playing with their toys or through one or other of the graphic arts. One reason for the inclusion of art work in schools, then, is simply to ensure that all children have adequate opportunity of this kind.

2. As it happens, the limitation of children's creative activity occurs at a time when the visual world is fresh and is seen with startling clarity and wonder. Children enjoy looking at things, and the best language for expressing what they see is naturally through the use of drawing, painting or modelling. This leads us to a second reason for the inclusion of art in education, namely that it is important for us all to have command over the language of colour and form so that we can convey thoughts, or information, which cannot easily be expressed in words or through any other means of communication.

Our eyes can be a source of pleasure and stimulation at all times and they are the most useful of our senses. It is unfortunate that visual education has been neglected for so long and that so few adults have learned to use their eyes except for such purposes as steering cars or counting change. Vision and expression are closely related; if nothing is ever expressed then little is really seen, and, of course, if nothing is seen then there is nothing to express. Continual use of the graphic arts from childhood onwards could ensure that the clarity and intensity of a child's observation are continued into adult life.

3. For young children below the age of seven or eight expressing what they see in the external world is probably less important than expressing what they see in their own unconscious inner worlds. This aspect of art has been the subject of much research over the last half-century and the results have been used with some success – even among adults – in psychotherapy. To give an extreme example; when a child is passing through a phase of night terrors, the parents can observe the beneficial result if the child can be encouraged to talk of the vision and then to paint or model it. The act of creating a tangible image puts the mind outside the vision so that a rational attitude replaces the fear.

Mother, baby, pram and dog by a five-year-old child

It is interesting to note the similarity of subject matter in the pictures or models of most young children, and to see that it is so often drawn from the comforts of their environment. Most children are capable of modelling around the age of three and will produce such things as plates of food, babies in cots, prams, or token images of their mothers. Similar ideas will be noticed in the art of primitive cave dwellers who were dependent on animals for their food and clothing, and who were in constant danger from wild beasts.

4. A fourth reason for the inclusion of art in education is that consciousness of the visual world induces a critical attitude to its appearance. This is an important part of the development of personality. A critical observer does not buy ugly things or choose to live among squalid surroundings, nor, more important, does he make the environment of everybody else squalid by, for example, the erection of shoddy buildings or by wantonly destroying natural beauty. If all adults were sensitive observers, our towns and countryside would present a very different picture, and the result in terms of dignity, efficiency and spiritual and physical health would amply repay the increased expenditure on art or craft facilities.

In relation to this aim it is necessary that children should encounter, and use, many different materials. Ideas of line, colour and texture may well be expressed in pencil or paint, but few children attain sufficient mastery over these media to experience also ideas of three-dimensional form and the balance that exists between purpose, process and material in design. Craftwork of many kinds can fulfil this purpose.

5. A fifth use of art and craft facilities may be mentioned if only because, in principle, it embodies the same inter-relationship between vision and expression as did the second aim. This is the use of painting or craftwork to help with the digestion of knowledge. Learning is not an easy process and the act of painting a picture or making a model of some topic is an effective means of translating passive absorption into active participation. There is an old saying *No Impression Without Expression* which summarizes this approach succinctly. The means of expression need not always be visual, but it will be found that the most effective teaching often occurs through these means because of the superiority of the senses of sight and touch.

No subject can be studied in isolation. The crafts are inevitably practised in studios away from other classrooms, but they will lose their value if their influence does not extend beyond the studio walls. Chapters 2 and 3 of this book, 'Origins' and 'Clay and Man', show how pottery is related to, and is an essential part of, every aspect of civilized life from its very earliest beginnings.

How can these aims be successfully carried out?

In the first place it would seem necessary for the children or students to learn the techniques of the craft before they can do anything with it, and a graduated series of exercises, calculated to make them familiar with every detail of each process, can easily be made out. This approach is certainly logical and has been a feature of craft teaching for many years. The fact remains that it rarely seems to work and in the majority of cases it kills any aptitude for craftwork more surely than any other means. The weakness of the approach is that it puts the importance of technique before the expression of ideas, and thus impedes the natural incentives of exploration and personal discovery. It is a reasonable approach to industrial apprenticeship or courses where ideas are of secondary importance and, as a method of teaching, it seems the only sensible one to employ when giving instruction in the use of dangerous machinery or weapons.

When children first encounter a harmless block of plastic clay, however, they will play with it for some time by banging it, rolling it, pulling it apart and smearing it together again. If there is a stick or some other tool within reach they will use it as a prodder and scratcher. With children of nursery school age this process may be repeated on numerous occasions before anything constructive is made, but ultimately they will want to give form to ideas and may seek advice on the manipulation of the material. A skilled craft teacher will be able to ensure that ideas and technical ability grow together.

Children have ideas of their own in plenty stemming from their subconscious worlds as well as from their intense observation of the visual one that surrounds them, but they need

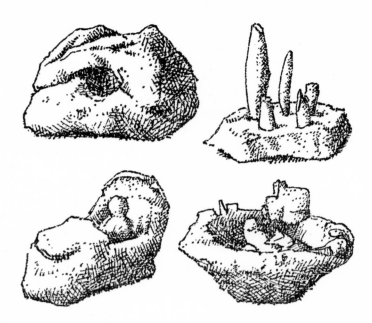

Typical models by pre-school age children. *Top left:* early experiment built up by smearing layer upon layer of small pieces together by a child aged three. *Top right:* another model by the same child made a month or so later. It was said to represent candles on a cake and shows considerable advance in control of the material acquired without direct instruction. *Bottom left:* work of a four-year-old. *Bottom right:* the first representation of nature by a three-year-old, made immediately after watching birds in a nest. The technique of pinching a bowl form was discovered afresh by this child in the attempt to produce a suitable form for a nest

help to crystallize these images one at a time, or to isolate any one image for long enough to turn it into a model or picture. This help can be given by questioning the child about the important details of what he says he intends to depict, or it can be done in a class by a vivid description of something that is within the realm of the childrens' experience. By such means the images are enclosed within frames so that a picture appears in the mind where once there was a dancing succession of panoramic views or incidents.

The processes of narrowing and sharpening personal images before they are given tangible form in modelling or some other medium demand careful study because it is the key to successful art teaching with all ages. It can lead to the enforcement of the teacher's own ideas upon the children, but it should, in fact, be the freeing of their own, and is the essence of what has been called the 'New Art Teaching' or 'Free-expression'. To describe in words the compact, massive form of an elephant, for instance, with its wrinkled skin, flappy ears, tusks, trunk, narrow beam and dignified rhythmical movement, recalls to the mind of the listener their own personal image. On the other hand to draw such a beast on the blackboard presents immediately a ready-made image which will be copied without further thought or reference to personal experience. Those readers who feel hesitant about this aspect of art teaching would be well advised to read some of the books listed in the bibliography on teaching, especially those by Marion Richardson and Sybil Marshall.

Free-expression is sometimes thought to be a continual invitation to paint or model 'anything you like' thrown out to each group of students as they enter the studio, but such freedom is intolerable to most children because they cannot decide which of their many images to put down first, with the result that their creative urges are paralysed. Free-expression is also a label that is sometimes mistakenly applied to abstract art.

With ideas established and growing apace the teacher will find himself busy giving technical advice and assistance to small groups or individuals. He will need to show them how to make flat sheets of clay without them sticking to the bench, and to stick one piece of clay to another so that they do not come apart in the fire. What he says to one child will be noted by the next and a sound tradition of working methods will grow unconsciously. The range of techniques can be slowly extended by the kind of ideas suggested; at the start the images called forth may be small and of a character that could be modelled from short coils and small pieces on a flattened disc of clay (Plates 25 and 26). Later, as skill increases, they can be extended in scope so that it is felt necessary for them to be modelled larger, and therefore hollow, by the use of clay strips or sheets (Plates 23 and 24).

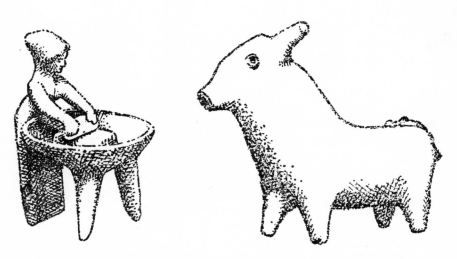

Laundress, 450 B.C. and bull, approximately 1700 B.C. made by natural rolling and pinching techniques

Children welcome sincere and honest criticism, but it must always be given with their age and personal capability in mind. It must be remembered that children do not begin to see in anything like an adult way until they are eight or ten years old. Prior to this age they depict what they know rather than what they see; for example, when painting several figures seated round a table they may well show the legs and chairs of those seated at the far side, and possibly the whole scene in plan. There comes a time when this apparent oddity of vision is realized by the child and help will be demanded to make the pictures or models more convincing.

Attempts to enforce adult vision before such advice is asked for are sure to upset the child's confidence in the rightness of what he is doing and may well make him unwilling to venture further into the world of visual expression, consequently impairing his enjoyment of visual experience. This is a serious tragedy that has already happened to most of us, and probably accounts for the 'blindness' of many adults more than any particular lack of opportunity for visual expression in youth or childhood. The old methods of art teaching with their emphasis on proficiency in copying superficial appearances did untold harm, but so do we today, indirectly, by encouraging the sale of pictures executed by numbers, embroidery stencils, rubber moulds for figures and many other forms of copying material. In all these prefabrications the images are adult; they set children a criterion for art work which is alien to their natures and often poor in itself.

The child whose confidence has been lost is unfortunately a familiar sight in art classes. What can be done for him? He can, perhaps, be taught to look afresh for himself; it may even help to draw or model something for him, explaining all the time that one is looking hard at every feature of the object before you so that he is left in no doubt that drawing and modelling are largely based on observation, and are not tricks or inaccessible skills. Before long he may join in and be eagerly discovering things for himself.

There is little that can be added to these general remarks about the teaching of pottery itself. The arrangement of studios and the particular emphasis of the work are matters which can only be decided by individuals to suit their own circumstances and temperaments.

Specific guidance is given in Part Three about clays, kilns and other materials because beginners cannot order their first supplies from their own experience, and there is little opportunity for them to inspect goods beforehand. The needs of industry, small workshops or craftrooms in schools are very different, and the suppliers who deal with all three do not always appreciate the problems of the schools. Industrialists may look askance at a clumsy pot with a crazed glaze forgetting that the true value of it does not lie in the pot itself, but in the stimulation of creating it and what has been learned during the process. If the recipe of the crazed glaze was worked out by the student himself it will not be long before he learns to correct the fault, which is a very different matter from never encountering the problem because he has used, from the first instance, the superlative materials industry is capable of supplying.

The choice of a suitable clay is of paramount importance. Many first excursions into pottery have been spoiled by the purchase of white slimy clay such as that used for the machine production of tableware, or what industry calls 'modelling clay' which is almost as smooth. It is obviously desirable to obtain as much clay as possible from local sources, but the labour and time involved have to be balanced against the loss of making time, and each potter will decide for himself whether or not it is worthwhile. The quantities of clay required by any studio or school will vary from a few pounds to a few tons, and it is difficult to keep large quantities in a suitable condition for use as scrap clay may accumulate faster than pots. One method of storage and re-conditioning is outlined between pages 76 and 78.

Glazes of all kinds and colours can be bought ready prepared, but the creation of one's own recipes from raw materials is much more exciting. Even more interesting is the search for the raw materials themselves which soon exposes gaps in our knowledge of the Earth that can only be filled by an elementary study of geology. This is fortunately an attractive open-air science requiring little in the way of equipment and about which some very readable books have been written. It is surprising that this subject is often neglected in schools because it forms a useful practical link between chemistry, physics, biology, geography, environmental studies and, to some extent, astronomy.

However far it is taken, an experimental approach to glazes – and clays – engenders a higher pitch of enthusiasm, and breeds a far deeper understanding of the craft, than rows of brown paper packets will ever do. As an example, the Buttermere slate glaze applied to the pot in plate 20 was discovered by a group of students who had collected pebbles from a Solway beach. The pebbles were fired to various temperatures and on examination of the results it was found that a pale greenish one had flowed out to a smooth black glass at 1300° C. It did not take long to decide that this pebble was a chip of local slate and, as one student of the group lived near the quarries, a supply of sludge from the sawing machinery was soon acquired which, with slight additions, made an excellent glaze. Similar results, though with more additions, were also achieved from granites.

After these introductory experiments with raw materials these students followed a normal course of training which included also some work on kilns and Raku ware. Eventually it was decided that they needed to be more independent and the usual services provided by any pottery department – buckets of glaze, firings, etc. – were withdrawn from them so that they were forced to plan and carry out every stage of their work for themselves. The results of this treatment were so remarkable that it was finally decided that they would benefit by building their own kiln and making their own wheel if they wanted to throw.

Bibliography to Chapter 1

Books About Art Teaching and the Art Work of Children

Sybil Marshall, AN EXPERIMENT IN EDUCATION. *Cambridge University Press, 1st and 2nd editions 1963.* This highly recommended book concerns the whole of education. Its author was a virtually untrained teacher when she took charge of a one-teacher village school in Cambridgeshire at the beginning of the war. As the years went on she slowly developed her own methods of opening the eyes and minds of children of all ages and all types; art of all kinds became the foundation of her teaching. The book is partly a diary of the author's 18 years at this school, but her methods are explained in detail and there are many illustrations of the results. The author is now a lecturer in Education at Sheffield University.

Marion Richardson, ART AND THE CHILD. *University of London Press 1948 (5th impression 1964).* Like Sybil Marshall's book this is, in part, a diary covering the important years of the author's life between the two wars, and it is equally recommended. After a dozen or more years of teaching in various schools Miss Richardson became Inspector of Schools under the London County Council, and did much to spread the gospel of what she calls the New Art Teaching. This book gives a clear insight into her methods of drawing the best art work from children, and it gives an idea of their needs. Examples are illustrated, many in colour.

Wilhelm Viola, CHILD ART AND FRANZ CIZEK. *Austrian Junior Red Cross, Vienna 1936.* Cizek not only established a new form of art teaching, but was the first to realize the importance of 'Child Art' in any shape or form. He made his discoveries in 1885 and opened his internationally famous Juvenile Art Class in 1896. This book is an historical record of this pioneering work; it records Cizek's ideas in detail, and contains many illustrations of the work produced and the classes at work. Cizek believed that once a child's creative power has been developed his whole outlook on life will be influenced by it.

Wilhelm Viola, CHILD ART. *University of London Press, 2nd edition 1944.* This book explains exactly what child art is and the way it grows; it discusses the part that teachers and parents have to play, and clears up many misconceptions about childrens' work that arose during the early days of the 'New Art Teaching' in Britain. Since 1934 the author has been lecturing here and part of the book is occupied by answers to typical questions that teachers asked after his talks – this is useful in that the same questions are still, and always will be, asked. The latter half of the book is taken up with verbatim accounts of some lessons given by Cizek himself. There are a few illustrations in black and white, but unfortunately the book is a war economy production.

R. R. Tomlinson, PICTURE MAKING BY CHILDREN. *Studio 1934.* R. R. Tomlinson was Senior Inspector of Art for the London County Council and was Marion Richardson's chief. This book is especially valuable in that it is illustrated by examples from all over the world which are clearly marked with size, medium, age and often the source of inspiration. The many illustrations are accompanied by a detailed and authoritative text.

R. R. Tomlinson, CRAFTS FOR CHILDREN. *Studio 1935.* Like Tomlinson's previous volume the examples in this book are from all over the world and its text is invaluable.

R. R. Tomlinson, CHILDREN AS ARTISTS. *King Penguin 1944.* A brief and explicit statement of the history and aims of art teaching.

S. M. Robertson, CREATIVE CRAFTS IN EDUCATION. *Routledge and Kegan Paul, 5th impression 1964.* Though this book pays much attention to tools, methods and materials involved in many crafts – including pottery and modelling – its major contribution lies in the author's philosophical discussions on teaching, the characteristics of children of all ages and the place of crafts in our society. Methods are illustrated by drawings and there are 24 interesting photographs.

Ruth Dunnett, ART AND CHILD PERSONALITY. *Methuen and Co. 1948.* An absorbing account of the art and craftwork carried out in a temporary camp secondary school between 1940 and 1945. The author explains how the work grew to be an important activity in the school, and how her own teaching methods developed along with it.

Kenneth Holmes and Hugh Collinson, CHILD ART GROWS UP. *Studio 1952.* A suggested approach to art and craftwork in schools. Illustrated with typical examples of work by children of all ages which are clearly labelled. It covers the appreciation of pictures, objective drawing, lettering and the co-ordination of art and craft subjects with the rest of the school curriculum. The text is brief and to the point.

Seonaid M. Robertson, CRAFTS AND CONTEMPORARY CULTURE. *U.N.E.S.C.O. Harrap 1961.* A series of thoughtful studies on the aesthetic, psychological and sociological aspects of craftwork in schools, colleges, rural workshops and industry. This book was commissioned by U.N.E.S.C.O. after a seminar on Art and Crafts in General Education and Community Life conducted at Tokyo in 1954. It quotes examples and experiences from all over the world and from all types of communities.

The framework of our educational system and the content of many other courses besides art and craft have been sharply criticized in recent times. It is evident that radical reform is necessary before the system can be considered adequate to meet the needs of forthcoming generations, and the following books or pamphlets are listed to show the trend of current opinion. There can be few art or craft teachers who would not welcome at least some of the recommendations.

H. Davies, Director of Nottingham University Institute of Education, THE CHANGING GRAMMAR SCHOOL. Nottingham University Educational Paper No. 2 (2/6d. + 3d. post). A forthright and brief assessment of the changes taking place – and required – in grammar schools. General Certificate of Education 'O' level is described as an 'incubus and educational catastrophe', and other features of the present system – streaming, 11 +, 6th form organization – are roundly criticized.

M. Hutchinson & C. Young, EDUCATING THE INTELLIGENT. *Pelican 1962.* A discussion of the educational needs of the top 40% of the intelligence range of our children. Suggestions for reform are made on curricula, examinations, 6th form study, university selection and the organization of the teaching profession.

John Vaizey, Director of an Educational Research Unit of London University, EDUCATION FOR TOMORROW. *Penguin Special 1962.* A broad examination of the entire system with suggestions about selection, types of school, teacher training and organization, administration and financing which would enable it to cope with the modern world.

John Hemming, TEACH THEM TO LIVE. *Longmans 1957.* A report on the long-term results of an experiment conducted in the 1930s by 30 American schools in conjunction with some universities. The object of the experiment was to replace a General Certificate of Education type university entrance examination by a method of selection which gave the schools freedom to devise their own syllabuses and methods of teaching.

John Blackie, GOOD ENOUGH FOR THE CHILDREN. *Faber and Faber 1963.* A collection of essays illuminated by a wide and practical experience of schools and a deep understanding of the real nature of education and the teacher's art.

Brian Jackson, STREAMING: AN EDUCATION SYSTEM IN MINIATURE. *Routledge and Kegan Paul 1964.* A well-reasoned argument, soundly based on statistical information specially collected, on the irrelevance of an academic practice in schools aiming at providing an equal educational opportunity for all.

J. W. B. Douglas, THE HOME AND THE SCHOOL. *MacGibbon and Kee 1964.* A study of our pupils, the accidental advantages and disadvantages of their home backgrounds, and a timely warning on the unconscious prejudices of many teachers.

PART TWO

Chapter 2

Origins

This chapter describes in brief outline the progress of a particle of energy from its original situation in the centre of the Universe, countless millions of years ago, until it becomes united with others as matter in the wall of a pot being made today. The story of its various transmutations is long and complicated and rather wonderful. It crosses and recrosses the boundaries between one science and another, unifying them as it develops, until nature is seen as a whole.

The full sweep of this story can only be hinted at in one chapter, but it is hoped that a coherent thread will emerge which could, if desired, be extended in depth from the books on separate topics listed at the end.

One can start from the clay end of the story and work backwards as the scientists themselves have done, or one could start from the beginning, out in space, and work forwards. In working backwards one has the advantage of starting with something that is tangible and which can be grasped. At the other end one encounters phenomena which are beyond immediate comprehension because our language is barely adequate to describe the sizes, distances, times and temperatures involved.

CLAY AND THE CHEMICAL ELEMENTS

Like all other substances clay is a chemical compound made up in a distinctive way from atoms of several elements. The atoms are not merely mixed together in a suitable proportion as a cake recipe is weighed into a bowl, but they are combined in an orderly pattern which, in solid substances, is reflected in the visible shape of its crystals, and which is the cause of such physical properties as plasticity, hardness, tensile strength and brittleness. These three-dimensional patterns are familiar to us from enlarged models or diagrams, and have become the stock-in-trade of artists designing for scientific publications.

Every solid substance has its own pattern which disappears when the substance is melted, though it will often reappear again on cooling. Liquids and gases have no crystal pattern, and it follows that if a solid does not regain some of its original pattern after melting, then it is likely to have some of the characteristics of a liquid – even transparency – because there are no crystal surfaces to reflect and interrupt the passage of light rays. Glass or glazes come into this category. They are often classified as 'super cooled' liquids to distinguish them from crystalline solids or other forms of matter.

The atoms involved in a molecule of pure clay – though such a substance does not exist in nature – are those of hydrogen, oxygen, aluminium and silicon. They are combined in such a way that clay consists of minute flat hexagonal crystals which slide about on one another like pieces of plate glass with water between them acting as a lubricant. The lubricant, or 'water of plasticity', is free to dry away and be replaced; when it has gone the clay is no longer plastic.

One feature of the clay molecules which is immediately noticeable is that it contains atoms of two gases and two metals, the properties of which become radically altered in combination. This change is a feature of all compounds, and molecules grow in an infinite variety of ways to form all the different kinds of organic or inorganic matter within and around us. The mechanism of this growth is an important study; in some molecules such as those of clay, the atoms are difficult to separate from one another; in other cases they may be readily parted and recombined into different compounds by the action of heat or substances like acids. Sometimes when atoms combine together heat is given off as in the instances of hydrogen or carbon combining with oxygen in the burning of oil, coal or wood.

The explanations for these phenomena lie within the atoms themselves. If atoms were really small solid spheres as they are depicted in molecular diagrams or models we should be at a loss to explain the cause of any reaction or property, but they have very complicated structures. In contrast to the molecules of compounds the atoms of all elements are constructed on the same basis and the same kinds of particles go to make up each. Their internal organization is similar to that of the solar system in which the Earth and eight other planets revolve around the Sun, held in place by its gravitational pull. In every atom there is a central nucleus around which other particles are held in orbit by electrical attraction and almost the entire internal volume in both the solar system or an atom consists of empty space.

With this emptiness in mind it is no longer easy to comprehend the weight of much of our surroundings, but atoms are very small indeed – a gram of hydrogen gas contains about 1 million, million, million, million of them! Solidity is also difficult to comprehend when it is known that there is so much movement going on all the time in any material, but it is the result of the strength of attraction between one atom and another, and then, as we have noted, from the kind of pattern in which the molecules are combined to form crystals. There is little bond between the molecules in a liquid, and none in a gas.

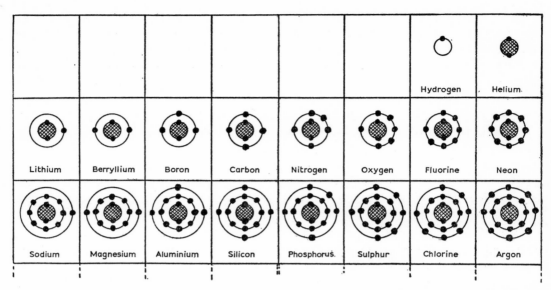

Part of the Periodic Table of the Elements showing the ascending number of electrons in the atoms

A little is known about the construction of atomic nuclei. The simplest nucleus contains one positively charged particle, known as a proton, which is balanced by one negatively charged orbiting electron giving a stable atom of the gas hydrogen. Other elements are created by increasing the number of protons present in the nucleus and also the number of orbiting electrons which balance them. The next element to hydrogen is helium whose atoms contain a pair of each particle; next come lithium with three of each and beryllium with four of each. So it goes on through the 92 elements of nature and the 102 of the full list.

A list of the elements organized in ascending order of the number of protons and electrons contained in their atoms is much more useful than one which is merely in alphabetical order because the names are arbitrary: some of them are ancient whilst others are derived from the names of scientists or places. Had all the elements been discovered at once we should doubtless have used numbers rather than names; as it is we use both.

During the nineteenth century several chemists realized that when the known elements were listed in order of complexity they occurred in groups having similar characteristics. After several attempts the Periodic Table of the Elements table was organized in which the list was broken down into nine vertical columns and seven horizontal ones. With some knowledge of this table it becomes possible to predict chemical and physical properties of the elements from the position in which they appear. Before all the elements were known the properties of the unknown ones were predicted by the positions of the blank squares, and these predictions have proved to be true.

One of the factors determining the number of columns used in the Periodic Table is the arrangement of the electrons. The orbits of the electrons are not haphazard and they follow similar paths in all the elements. For instance, hydrogen has one electron orbiting at a certain distance from its proton and helium has two electrons orbiting at this same distance. The next element, lithium, has three orbits, two of which are the same as helium and the third being some distance further away. Beryllium also has the inner orbits of helium and two in the more distant layer. In magnesium, which is element number 12, the pair of helium electrons are still present, a second layer contains eight, and there are two more in a third layer.

It is the outermost shell of electrons which governs the chemical properties of an atom, and those having less than eight in this layer seek to make the number up by combining with atoms of another element (those already having eight are inert). Sometimes atoms with only one or two electrons in their outer layers present them to those of other elements which are short by the same number, so that in the combined molecule both have complete outer layers (electrovalent). A stronger bond between atoms is made, however, when the outer layers lock together and share the electrons in order to complete one whole circuit (covalent). The stability of a chemical compound depends entirely on the method of bonding involved and it happens that the four elements making up the clay molecules bind well together.

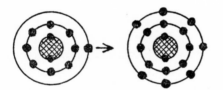 

Left: simple electrovalent bonding of sodium and chlorine atoms (salt).
Right: covalent bonding of two atoms of hydrogen and one of oxygen (water)

The clay molecule is complicated, consisting not of a single atom of each element involved, but of two atoms of aluminium, two of silicon, four of hydrogen and nine of oxygen. Oxygen, with six electrons in its outer layer, is a specially reactive element, and, as there is so much of it about the world, many atoms of other elements have already combined with it to form oxides. Clay is in reality not a compound of four separate elements, but a compound of three oxides; aluminium oxide (alumina), silicon oxide (silica), and hydrogen oxide (water), thus: $Al_2O_3 . 2SiO_2 . 2H_2O$.

It is now possible to see some of the reasons why ceramic goods are so resistant to chemical attack, and why they do not burn in the kiln. Ceramic molecules are well bonded and have above average stability. There is also a predominance of oxygen in the molecules already so that further additions of this, or any other gas from the atmosphere, even under conditions of intense heat when all elements are most reactive, are unacceptable into the pattern. No metals have either of these qualities to any comparable extent, nor do any of the other materials used by man for manufacturing purposes.

These splendid properties of ceramic materials are used to the full in the refractory industry which supplies furnace linings for almost every other industry. To some of our major industries such as steel making, cement making, glass and oil refining, ceramic refractory materials represent the life blood. In passing, it is interesting to note that the melting points of metallic oxides are often three or four times as high as those of the metals on their own, for instance, aluminium melts at 660° C. whilst the oxide does not do so until a temperature of 2050° C. has been reached. Other noticeable examples are calcium 852° C., oxide 2570° C.; sodium 98° C. oxide 600° C. – 700° C.; potassium 64° C. oxide 600° C. – 700° C. and magnesium 649° C. the oxide 2800° C.

THE EARTH AND THE UNIVERSE

With this brief glimpse of atomic structures fresh in our minds, some light may now be cast on the origin of the Earth itself. The following pages contain ideas which are mostly hypothetical, but they represent some current opinions in scientific circles. There is sufficient evidence to support them though there is nothing to say that they will not be changed as more becomes available.

As all sub-atomic particles are alike, it is conceivable that, given certain conditions, any element may be created at will, or that one may be made from another by the addition or subtraction of the appropriate particles. In ordinary industrial processes the elements are stable and cannot be transmuted, but it is becoming increasingly common for this to be done in the laboratory. With the equipment available at the moment it is easier to break a large atom into smaller ones than is the reverse operation, hence most nuclear reactions set off by man involve the use of the heaviest naturally occurring element – uranium. However, there are forces available in the Universe which make it possible to start from the other end of the scale and to build all the terrestrial elements from the lightest, which is hydrogen.

The geography of the Universe is on a scale which defeats imagination. We talk glibly of distances such as that which light travelling at 186,000 miles per second may travel in one year, but even these measurements are grossly inadequate in relation to the Universe when it is known to be expanding at a similar speed, or even faster. For this reason, among others, we shall never know all that is to be known about the Universe, and perhaps it would be as well to say here that there are also obstacles which bar us from ever knowing all that goes on inside the atom.

It appears that the Universe consists of nothing more than a sparse collection of hydrogen atoms; barely one atom to a cubic foot of space. In view of the figure quoted on page 33 for a normal number of atoms per gram of the gas, hydrogen in this concentration might appear to be a rare element, but the immensity of the volume of the Universe ensures that this is not so. The most powerful telescope in existence at Palomar Mountain in America can observe stars at a distance of 5,000 million light years away, and this is known to be only a fraction of the ultimate size.

All these atoms of hydrogen are turning slowly round a central point, and when a volume of gas behaves in this fashion it inevitably happens that smaller eddies appear at various points in which the sparse atoms accumulate more thickly. These eddies of hydrogen where the atoms have accumulated form the basis of what we call galaxies, of which there are some 1,000 million in observable space. As one may imagine, the galactic eddies also revolve and again form smaller eddies within themselves in which the hydrogen atoms reach a degree of concentration sufficient to be termed a mass, and which is dense enough to generate a field of gravitational attraction drawing more and more atoms into itself, until the central core is subjected to very real pressure from the huge bulk of matter surrounding it.

With the increase of pressure the internal temperature begins to rise until it reaches a point around the 20 million° C. mark where thermonuclear reactions occur in which hydrogen is converted into the gas helium with the release of quantities of radiant energy. The active, super hot, mass is then a fully fledged star which will be visible throughout much of the Universe.

In overlarge stars the internal pressure and heat eventually become excessive, and atoms of greater and greater complexity are manufactured until finally the whole mass explodes like an atomic bomb, though on a scale which makes even the largest of man-made weapons appear rather less than a child's cap pistol. These exploding stars – known as supernovae – are rare indeed, but sufficient have occurred, and been observed, to ensure that in most galaxies there exists a small proportion of atoms heavier than hydrogen which are mixed into each eddying mass evolving into a star.

Just before the temperature of a star becomes sufficient to become reactive, the mass assumes a flattened disk shape because of the speed of rotation. The heavier atoms among the mass work out towards the edge where they follow the established routine by accumulating and finally forming solid balls which are left behind as the gases condense. Several accumulations of dense matter may be born in this way to any star. The Sun is a small star formed in this manner some 15,000 million years ago, and the Earth and eight other planets are its offshoots of solid matter formed before it became luminous. These nine bodies, or planets, and the Sun form what we call the solar system, situated towards the edge of our own galaxy. The Galaxy is between 60,000 and 100,000 light years across.

Galaxies and stars with their planetary systems are being born all the time. The process has been observed in various stages throughout the Universe, and the speeds with which the newly formed galaxies move away from the centre of the Universe have in some cases been measured. One has to keep in mind the scale of time involved and its relation to distance; no star in our own Galaxy is nearer to us than 25 million million miles, so that the image through a telescope is not what is taking place at the moment, but what in this case took place three years ago, and, in other cases, anything up to 50 million years ago. As there are upwards of 1,000 million visible galaxies known, each of which may contain anything up to 1,000 million stars, it would seem that the birth of a new star by the process described has every chance of being 'frequent'.

One last link is missing from this hypothesis of the nature of the Universe. We have a picture of eddies of hydrogen gas continually providing the material for more and more galaxies which rush away into space as soon as they are formed. When will the supply of hydrogen cease? The only reasonable answer to fit all the facts before us seems to be *never!* Somewhere in the centre of the Universe forces outside our comprehension must exist which are capable of not merely transmuting hydrogen into helium, but of making hydrogen itself.

So long as one retains an image of atoms, protons or electrons as being minute spherical particles of matter, the supposition that hydrogen can be generated spontaneously will not appear credible, but it has been proved consistently in recent years that matter is not so tangible. Protons, electrons, and all the other sub-atomic particles which, for the sake of simplicity, are not mentioned here are, in fact, condensed forms of energy.

The clay of a pot is but a congealed mass of X-rays, gamma-rays, beta-rays, electricity, light and so forth, equal, according to Einstein, to the weight multiplied *by the square of speed of light!*

One part of Einstein's theory could be seen to be true if only one could weigh all the gases produced from the fuel used in a firing. One would think that the weight of the exhaust gases would be equal to the weight of the fuel plus the amount of oxygen used to burn it, because, according to the rules of chemistry, nothing is lost in the process. But this is not so. An infinitesimally small fraction of weight is, in fact, lost in the burning process and it represents the weight of the heat supplied. Heat and matter are one and the same thing; each day man converts quantities of matter into energy, is it not conceivable that somewhere the reverse process should go on?

Is it any comfort to believe that we are not alone in this fantastic world of energy, space and time? Surely among the host of galaxies and their myriads of stars an odd hundred million or two attendant planets have reached a condition of development similar to our own and are supporting life – perhaps even potters!

THE CONTENTS OF THE EARTH

Unfortunately we cannot converse with our celestial counterparts, and, according to informed opinion, we are not likely to be able to do so as they are – if they exist at all – so far outside the solar system. Conditions outside the Earth do indeed form an absorbing study which is being explored very actively in this decade. It is probably true to say that we now know more about space than we do of our own world. However, the potter seeking clay has his feet firmly on the ground and will be wanting to know how the materials he uses evolved from the $\frac{1}{4}$% of the Sun's heavier elements that we inherited as a cloud of dust some 5,000 million years ago.

The eddy of heavy dust that was to form our Earth contracted finally into a spinning ball about 8,000 miles across. As the mass contracted the internal pressures increased, and, as the pressure rose, so likewise did the temperature, until it was sufficient to cause nuclear reactions which have assisted in maintaining to this day a temperature of about 5000° C. in the inner core.

Long before the temperature reached 5000° C. the mass melted and the heaviest elements settled towards the centre. It is now suspected that the central core of the Earth – some 5,000 miles across – consists of liquid metals with, perhaps, a solid core of iron and nickel which is thought to be the source of the Earth's magnetic field. The outer layers of the Earth, averaging 1,000 miles in thickness, consist for the most part of hard rock formations and are the ones with which we are specially concerned.

The composition of the outer layers has also been determined by the same force which initially drew the metals into the core. This force, known as gravity, cannot yet be entirely explained, but it is known that masses attract one another, and that the larger the mass the greater is the attraction exerted towards a smaller one.

In the outer layers of the Earth the 92 naturally occurring elements are found in varied proportions, only eight of them being present in amounts larger than 1%. The commonest element is oxygen which accounts for nearly half the total composition of these layers. Oxygen is not present in gaseous form, but occurs, as it does in clay, in combination with all the other 91 elements in the list, hence a percentage list of oxides tells more of the Earth's composition than one of the elements alone. When this list is compared with analyses of various ceramic materials such as glazes, clays, enamels (or even glass and cement which can be included under the same heading) it becomes evident that the relationship between pottery and the Earth is much closer than the mere fact that clay is dug from the ground would suggest. Overleaf is a table showing the proportions in which the eight commonest elements and their oxides occur in the crust, together with analyses of ceramic materials for comparison.

These seven common oxides – and of course the other eighty-four, as well as chlorides, sulphides, etc. – are present in very complicated crystal formations known as minerals. There is much speculation about the way in which the many different types of rock have been formed from these minerals, but the most acceptable theory at the moment appears to be that propounded by Professor Bowen in 1936. Starting from the accepted fact that the Earth was once molten, Bowen proceeded to investigate the effect of slow cooling on a quantity of oxides present in roughly the proportion of Clarke's and Washington's averages. It became evident from Bowen's experiments that as they cooled the oxides began to unite into crystals of recognizable mineral substances.

In the first place some of the silica present in Bowen's experiments appeared to unite with the iron oxide and magnesia to form heavy crystals of 'ferromagnesian' minerals which sank to the bottom of the chamber. Later, more silica combined with lime, alumina, soda

Percentages of the eight commonest elements in the crust		Percentage of oxides present in the Earth's crust*		Percentage analyses of typical ceramic substances				
				1300°C Glaze	Red Clay	Glass	Enamel	Cement
Oxygen	46·5							
Silicon	27·6	Silica	59·1	60·7	59·6	58·0	56·0	23
Aluminium	8·1	Alumina	15·2	13·4	22·0	2·0	5·3	7
Iron	5·1	Iron oxide	6·8	—	6·6	2·0	—	3
Calcium	3·6	Lime	5·1	5·2	0·6	2·5	3·8	62
Sodium	2·8	Soda	3·7	2·3	0·8	4·0	8·7	—
Potassium	2·6	Potash	3·1	5·3	0·8	12·0	2·4	—
Magnesium	2·1	Magnesia	3·4	—	0·8	1·0	—	3
others	1·6		3·6	13·1	8·8	18·5	23·8	2

* These figures were worked out in 1924 by the American scientists F. W. Clarke and H. S. Washington by averaging over 5,000 analyses from all over the world.

and potash to form various felspars, or similar materials, and finally the excess silica crystallized on the top as quartz. The order of mineral formation which Bowen noted, together with the chemical composition of the minerals, is as follows:

1. Olivine	$2\, Feo.\, SiO_2$ or $2\, MgO.\, SiO_2$.
2. Calcium Felspar	$CaO.\, AI_2O_3.\, 2\, SiO_2$.
3. Pyroxene	$MgO.\, SiO_2$.
4. Biotite Mica	$(K_2.\, Mg.\, Fe.)\, O.\, AI_2O_3.\, 6\, SiO_2.\, 2\, H_2O$.
5. Orthoclase Felspar	$K_2O.\, AI_2O_3.\, 6\, SiO_2$.
6. Quartz	SiO_2.

However, the layers were not clearly defined, and the minerals were jumbled forming groups which correspond closely to the average composition of various well recognized rocks. Olivine, calcium felspar and pyroxene compose rocks known as peridotite and eclogite, and the minerals pyroxene, biotite mica and orthoclase felspar form the better known rock basalt. Finally, more mica, orthoclase felspar and quartz formed granite. These processes of rock formation could be clarified thus:

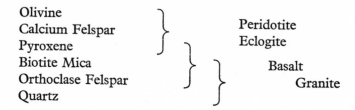

Olivine
Calcium Felspar
Pyroxene
Biotite Mica
Orthoclase Felspar
Quartz

Peridotite
Eclogite

Basalt
Granite

The four types of rock, peridotite, eclogite, basalt and granite do in fact form the outer 700-odd miles of thickness of the Earth with, of course, the heaviest ones towards the centre. A layer of basalt forms the foundation of the actual crust of the Earth, and granite forms the foundation of the landmasses. Most of the other kinds of rock known to us, including clay (see page 72), have been created by the slow decomposition of these two formations.

The forces of destruction at work on the outer crust – ice, wind, heat, water and dilute acids – have operated on a gigantic scale over a period of between 4 and 5,000 million years, and the science we know as geology has, until recently, been concerned almost entirely with unravelling the stages and effects of this onslaught.

However, we are not sure that peridotite and eclogite are the rocks forming the layer known as the Earth's mantle which occurs directly under the basalt. No man is certain that he has seen a specimen of rock from this layer which starts about 75 miles beneath the surface and descends to a depth of around 700 miles. In a very few places the crust is thought to be only two or three miles thick and an attempt is being made to drill through such a point by some American geologists led by Willard Bascom. Results from the project, known as Mohole, are eagerly awaited, but the difficulties of the operation are quite on a par with those involved in constructing a rocket to probe into space. (See Bascom's account of this venture, *A Hole in the Bottom of the Sea*, Weidenfeld & Nicolson 1962, which also contains a lucid survey of the extent of our geological knowledge.)

LAND AND LIFE

Bowen's ingenious experiments support other hypotheses about the shape and disposition of the land masses over the surface of the Earth. It has already been suggested that the cooling of the Earth has been complicated by continual reheating from within caused by nuclear fission, and this resulted in the molten rock magmas of the mantle and lower crust behaving like simmering jam in which light materials collect as patches of scum on top of convecting currents. The crust is now set and apparently rigid, but the rocks deep down in the mantle, where the temperature is high, are likely to be comparatively plastic. Very slow currents are presumed to move in these regions and, though the ascending material no longer reaches the surface, it moves slowly along underneath it before it again descends towards the centre. This action imparts a dragging movement underneath the crust which

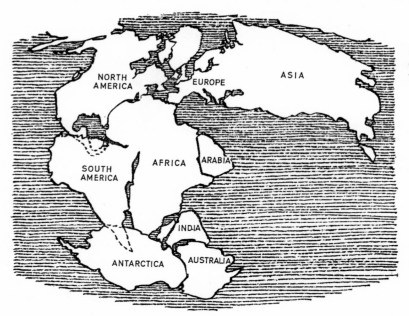

Suggested map of the original distribution of the landmasses

has been sufficient to slowly move whole continents of granite material over the surface of the globe at a rate of about an inch per year or 4,000 miles in 250 million years!

Geography starts from this point. There is good evidence to show that there was once only one, or possibly two, land masses which have been torn apart and dragged over the face of the Earth to their present dispositions by the action of these convecting currents. The shapes of the continents to-day would seem possibly to fit together like pieces of a jig-saw puzzle, and additional support for the theory that they were once united is given by the similar rock formations which are to be found on, for instance, the West coast of Africa and the East coast of South America. The direction of magnetic fields which set within the rock formations as they cooled also supports the theory of continental drift.

The Theory of Continental Drift was first put forward by Alfred Wegener who died in Greenland in 1930 whilst seeking further evidence to support it. The theory is accepted by many and a suggested map of the original geography of the Earth is shown above. It will be noticed that India is shown well down in the Southern Hemisphere and Africa is aligned West of Europe. It has also been suggested that, when these continents moved to their present positions, the impact of India against Asia caused the crust to buckle throwing up the Himalayas, and when Africa bumped Europe – before the Mediterranean Sea was enclosed – the Alps were thrown up.

Is it surprising that for a good two-thirds of its span of between 4 and 5,000 million years the Earth was not able to support even the simplest cellular forms of life?

Bibliography to Chapter 2

In order to read further into the wealth of subjects touched upon so briefly in this chapter there seems no need to look further than the splendid scientific books published in paperback editions.

Chemistry and the Nature of Matter

Alan Isaacs, INTRODUCING SCIENCE. *Pelican 1963*. A readable book of which the first half covers the laws governing the constitution of various types of matter; the second half discusses general concepts about energy, and its distinct forms in detail. The whole field is clearly related to ideas concerning the Earth and the Universe in an introduction and postscript.

Kenneth Hutton, CHEMISTRY. *Pelican (revised) 1961*. The first part of this excellent book provides a readable introduction to the whole field of chemistry; the second part – perhaps not so relevant to pottery – shows in a fascinating way how this science affects our lives and industry. Other topics discussed are fuels, food, clothes, plastics, drugs, disinfectants, explosives and radioactive tracers. A bibliography is included for each chapter.

R. J. Forbes & E. J. Dyksterhuis. A HISTORY OF SCIENCE AND TECHNOLOGY. *Pelican (2 vols.) 1963*. A broad history of the subjects containing much that is of great interest to the craftsman, though parts of both volumes are specialist material. Full bibliographies are given to each chapter.

David Abbott, THE STRUCTURE OF MATTER. *Pan Piper Science Series 1966*. A concise account written for the general reader and illustrated with many diagrams. The book covers the elements and their classification; solids, liquids and gases; atomic structure and energy; molecules, chemical linkage and reactivity; analysis by X-ray and electron diffraction. It contains also a useful glossary.

The Universe and the Creation

Fred Hoyle, THE NATURE OF THE UNIVERSE. *Pelican (revised) 1960*. Brief, most readable, and as absorbing as a first-class novel. It covers all aspects of the stars, the Sun, the Earth and other planets. Afterwards, Patrick Moore's SPACE IN THE SIXTIES (*Pelican*) will be read with interest.

W. M. Smart, THE ORIGIN OF THE EARTH. *Pelican (revised) 1959*. An account divided into three main sections, Whence?, When?, and How?, the book gives a lucid account of the whys and wherefores of this important event, with particular emphasis on the development of the various ideas held by previous generations. It aims to distinguish accepted theory from speculation or guesswork.

Other recommended Pelicans on the subjects of matter and the Universe:

Banesh Hoffmann, THE STRANGE STORY OF THE QUANTUM.

H. W. Newton, THE FACE OF THE SUN.

Stephen Toulmin & June Goodfield, THE FABRIC OF THE HEAVENS, also THE ARCHITECTURE OF MATTER.

A. R. Ubbelohde, MAN AND ENERGY.

James A. Coleman, RELATIVITY FOR THE LAYMAN.

The Structure of the Earth

H. H. Read, GEOLOGY. *Home University Library (No. 198), Oxford 1958.* Bound, but paperback in price and of inestimable value as a general study of the structure and history of the Earth. Illustrated with diagrams and including a detailed annotated bibliography.

H. H. Swinnerton, THE EARTH BENEATH US. *1955. (Pelican ed. 1958.)* An account of the Earth's structure and development with special emphasis on the causes of its present appearance and constitution. Good photographic illustrations and a few diagrams.

W. G. Tearnside & O. M. B. Bulman, GEOLOGY IN THE SERVICE OF MAN. *Pelican (revised) 1961.* A standard and readable textbook of the whole subject, including its application.

Regional Geology

L. Dudley Stamp, BRITAIN'S STRUCTURE AND SCENERY. *Fontana Library 1965.* Well-known general study of British scenery originally published in Collins' New Naturalist Series (1946) with many illustrations, but now available as a paperback without the original colour plates. Includes maps, diagrams and a very useful annotated bibliography.

A. E. Trueman, GEOLOGY AND SCENERY IN ENGLAND AND WALES. *1938. Pelican edition 1961.* Each chapter is devoted to a district of the British Isles; important features are discussed and illustrated with excellent line drawings, maps and diagrams – 95 in all.

Walter Shepherd, THE LIVING LANDSCAPE OF BRITAIN. *Faber and Faber 1952. Paperback edition 1963.* A clear study of scenery and its causes for the rambler in Britain. 80 excellent photographs; 150 diagrams, maps, etc., and bibliography.

Clarence Ellis, THE PEBBLES ON THE BEACH. *Faber and Faber 1954. Paperback edition 1965.* Perhaps skirting the edge of our problem, but there is a surprising amount to be learned from the beaches. Non-technical reading with some clear colour illustrations.

D. V. Ager, INTRODUCING GEOLOGY. *Faber and Faber* 1961. *Paperback edition* 1966. Discusses the evolution of that part of the Earth's crust which is now Britain. Well illustrated with maps, diagrams and photographs, and contains a glossary, bibliography and list of learned societies.

The most detailed regional surveys available are those published by H.M.S.O. for the Geological Survey and Museum. These are intended to be read in conjunction with the excellent series of maps (one inch to the mile, one quarter inch to the mile or ten miles to the inch) available from the same source.

Rocks and Minerals

W. R. Jones and David Williams, MINERALS AND MINERAL DEPOSITS. *Home University Library (No. 202.) Oxford 1960.* Another bound volume at paperback price covering the subject fully in a most interesting way. Chapters cover the physical and chemical character of minerals, location of deposits, methods of finding and extraction and economic importance. Contains also a useful glossary.

W. R. Jones, MINERALS IN INDUSTRY. *Pelican (revised) 1963.* An essential reference book in which much interesting information is given about the sources and uses of each element and its chief compounds. Arranged in alphabetical order and including maps showing the distribution of the chief minerals throughout the world. METALS IN THE SERVICE OF MAN. *(Pelican, revised 1954)* by H. Street and W. Alexander also provides interesting information about several of the 'ceramic' elements – especially aluminium. It also contains distribution maps.

Herbert S. Zim and Paul R. Shaffer, ROCKS AND MINERALS. *Paul Hamlyn, A Little Guide in Colour, 1965.* Clearly organized list illustrated throughout in colour and with informative text.

The best colour illustrations for those who are unfamiliar with the subject are to be found in ROCKS AND MINERALS by J. F. Kirkaldy. *Blandford Press 1963.*

Remains of a ziggurat

Chapter 3

Clay and Man

Clay is perhaps more useful to man than any other single substance, and the ease with which it can be shaped has led to its use for an astonishing variety of purposes in almost every community of which we have any trace. It has provided homes and palaces; it is cooked in and eaten off; it stores food and liquids; it provides the linings for domestic-sized stoves, industrial boilers or the huge interiors of modern blast furnaces, cement kilns and glass furnaces; it insulates electricity supplies and provides fundamental parts of internal combustion and rocket engines. Clay has also, ever since it was first discovered, been used as a medium of artistic expression. So widespread has been its use over such a long period of time that clay articles now provide the historian with his first knowledge of most races and a study of pottery history has become the background to the training of any archaeologist; pottery has, in fact, been called the 'alphabet of archaeology'.

The two factors which have helped the historian most are the fragility of claywares – hence their constant production – and the absolute permanence of them, whole or broken. The broken pot is discarded and its worthless pieces remain on the refuse tip, where they were thrown, to be dug out layer by layer and dated by their character or technique. So the story of many a race has been pieced together, their trading habits, their techno-logical development, their customs and their religions. Least expected, but most important, among these discoveries have been the earliest written records of man in the clay tablets and cylinders of the Sumerians and other races of Mesopotamia, of whom we now have more detailed records of daily life than almost any other people before or afterwards. Whole libraries have been discovered recording in detail business transactions, marriages, customs, ceremonies, laws and traditions.

The fundamental tie between man and clay offers as much to the teaching of history as does the study of clay technology offer to the teaching of science. The field of study is almost as vast as that covered by Chapter 2, and the pace of the next few pages will be equally rapid.

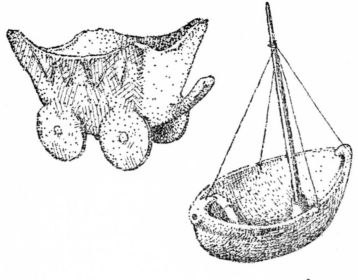

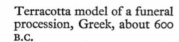

Clay articles provide the historian with important information. *Left:* a cart said to be the earliest known representation of a wheeled vehicle, about 2000 B.C. and a sailing boat also said to be the earliest known representation of such a vessel

Terracotta model of a funeral procession, Greek, about 600 B.C.

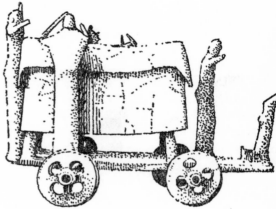

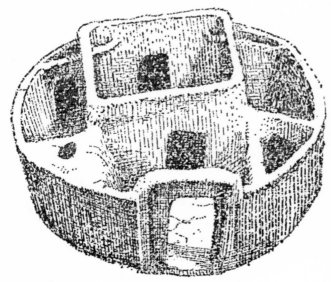

Model of a house about 2500 B.C. Diameter 21½ inches. Interesting both as a record and as an interpretation of a house in clay

BUILDING MATERIALS

Various forms of life, both animal and vegetable, have joined forces with ice, water, wind and the Sun in effecting considerable changes in the original surface of the Earth. We are amazed at huge tracts of ancient forests now buried deep down and changed into coal, and the great bulk of limestone mountains which were laid originally under the sea by the death of fantastic quantities of minute sea creatures, but has not man achieved much the same result with his rapacious desire for clay and other minerals?

Each hour in this island alone we make a million bricks; that is enough in a year to build a 10 foot-high-wall over a distance of some 25,000 miles – just once round the Earth. And one may look from many an English window to see almost nothing but the bricks of previous decades, those of the nineteenth century being particularly in evidence. In the early nineteenth century it took two and a half tons of coal to fire one ton of bricks and this ratio can only have been higher in earlier races – where wood was used it was likely to have been four or six tons of fuel to one of clay. Is it surprising, therefore, that the earliest major brick-building civilization – that of the Indus Valley – is thought to have turned its environment into a desert by the wholesale felling of trees for use as fuel?

The kilns of the Indus Valley were in active operation between the second and third millennia B.C. We know little in detail about these people because we cannot read their writing, but there are extensive remains of three large cities – Mohenjo-Daro, Harappa and Lothal – and many smaller ones in S.E. Pakistan which appear to have flourished between 2500 B.C. and 1500 B.C. These cities were built entirely of brick, and the larger ones occupied areas between six and seven square miles. They are among the earliest planned cities known to us and had most of the amenities that we know today including drainage, lavatories and fresh water supplies. The buildings were apparently undecorated, and the larger dwellings at least had many rooms (including swimming pools and showers) and courtyards which have set the pattern for living accommodation throughout India to the present day. Each city contained a central block which incorporated an elaborately ventilated grainstore, assembly halls, bath house and schools; at Mohenjo-Daro the grain store alone measures 164 feet by 82, and the entire citadel block some 400 feet by 200 by 50 feet high. At Lothal there is a brick-built dock measuring 700 feet by 120. In the mid-nineteenth century the remains of Harappa were largely destroyed when the bricks were re-used to provide over one hundred miles of foundation for the East India Railway between Karachi and Lahore.

The dates of the Indus civilization, which appears to have been finally terminated by invaders from the North, have been determined by the appearance of similar clay seals and stamps in the remains of Sumerian cities built beside another great river, the Euphrates. The Sumerians and all the later civilizations in this district also built with brick, though much of their work was sun-dried with only an outer casing of burned brickwork (Plate 1).

4

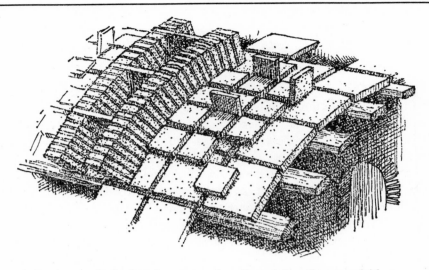

A Roman method of vault construction. Large clay tiles were laid over a light wooden shuttering and the joints were lapped by smaller ones, some of which were also stood on edge to prevent the superimposed concrete mixture from running down the curvature. Strengthening ribs were cast between double rows of tiles joined occasionally by larger ones

The central features of these cities were equally impressive, and we find at Uruk, Eridu, Aqar Quf, Khafage, Ur, Assur and Babylon the first attempts to provide residences for local gods. These residences took the form of terraced pyramids, or towers, known as ziggurats; in the case of Ur the measurements were 210 feet by 140 feet for the base with a height of 55 feet. Sun-dried brickwork has been identified at Jericho dating from the 6th millennium B.C.

The Greek builders used burned clay products only for roofing tiles, and the art of brickmaking did not enter Europe until the time of the Etruscans whose earliest efforts were possibly the walls of Arezzo. The Romans adopted the process during the reign of Julius Caesar and spread it throughout their Empire, as they did so many other building methods which are still in use today.

Roman buildings can be deceptive; they may appear to be brick or stone arched structures, but underneath they are often of monolithic cast concrete, uncomplicated by the requirements of thrust and counter-thrust found in those of the Gothic era. Roman concrete structures are the fruits of considerable advances in technology, and were made possible by the development of the Greek discovery of adding clay to limestone whilst it was being burned to produce mortar. At temperatures just below 1000° C. – which were some achievement in those times – the clay combined with the slaking lime producing insoluble calcium silicates and aluminates which are capable of not only resisting erosion by water, but of setting under it. Properly made from suitably selected materials such concrete is harder than many good building stones.

The Roman builders were not, however, content with the surface appearance of this magnificent building material, hence they faced their work with stone, marble or brick, and in most cases some brickwork was set in the concrete around arches to strengthen them whilst the cement hardened. Rectangular hollow-fired clay boxes were also set into larger vaults to lessen the deadweight and these were sometimes produced in voussoir shapes forming arches of various diameters. This practice was occasionally revived during the Renaissance and in later times; the Byzantine domes of S. Vitale and the baptistry at Ravenna are constructed entirely of interlocking earthenware jars and St. George's Hall in Liverpool, built in 1849, has one hundred and forty thousand square-sectioned hollow clay blocks set in its ceiling. Similar hollow blocks, generally 16 inches by 4, were also set by the Romans in walls and across vaults to conduct hot air from underfloor heating systems throughout the structure, giving the inhabitants a comfort not experienced again until the introduction of central heating in this century. In the tepidaria and caldaria of the great Roman bath-houses this heating system was especially useful in that it avoided cold condensed water vapour dropping from the roof on to the bathers. Such heating plants were known in Britain from about A.D. 80.

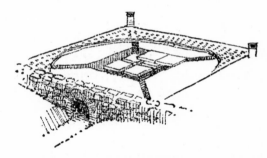

Left: hollow clay pots embedded in a Roman vault. *Right:* underfloor heating plant in a house at Verulamium

The crafts of brick and cement manufacture died in Europe with the Roman Empire, but brickmaking at least was kept going in the Near East from whence it spread back through the ports of Venice and Flanders nearly a thousand years later.

In Britain Roman bricks and tiles were re-used for some centuries, the tower of St. Alban's Abbey built between A.D. 1077 and A.D. 1115 being a famous example, and the craft of making new bricks was revived in East Anglia in the thirteenth century on the inspiration of the Low Countries. At first these new bricks were known as Flanders Tiles and the word 'brick' did not come into common use until Tudor times when the processes of manufacture were regulated in specific detail by an Act of Parliament (1477). Decorative bricklaying, using different colours and surface levels, was very popular at this time, but two hundred years later we find Wren setting a new standard of simplicity and elegance with his attractive combination of warm-coloured brickwork, white-painted window frames, doorways and cornices, which has lasted through till today. The craft spread to the U.S.A. in about A.D. 1600 and early examples exist in Richmond dating from 1611.

Various lime mortars and cements were used for jointing brickwork throughout the interval since the Roman Empire, but systematic research into structural possibilities of this material did not begin again until Robert Smeaton was faced with the problem of constructing the first Eddystone lighthouse in 1754. After many experiments he chose to use Aberthaw limestone and volcanic earth (pozzolana), such as the Romans themselves might have used, from Civita Vecchia in Italy. These experiments continued as the needs of industry grew and fairly reliable Portland cements, using siliceous clays, were being produced by I. E. Johnson at Swanscombe in Kent and Gateshead in 1845. Another Englishman of this period, Joseph Aspdin, realized that a better cement was produced if the entire carbon dioxide content of the mixture was driven off, but this could not be achieved without firing between 1400° C. and 1500° C., after which the sintered nodules required to be ground before use. Steel reinforcement rods were first incorporated by W. B. Wilkinson, one of Johnson's employees, in 1854.

In 1908 the French developed the black Ciment Fondu using aluminous materials – bauxite – instead of siliceous clays with the limestone. Fondu was developed initially to resist the strong sulphates in some ground waters, but, when it was discovered that it was quick setting and had a resistance to very high temperatures, it soon found applications in the steel and ceramic industries.

Ceramic tiles have as many uses as bricks, and, as towns grew in size in the Middle Ages, they became compulsory roofing materials in place of thatch or wood to prevent the spread of fire. In London they were made compulsory in A.D. 1212, though some towns, such as Norwich, did not take action until early in the sixteenth century.

There are three basic shapes of clay roofing-tile; curved tiles with narrower semi-circular sections inverted over the joints appeared in Greece in the seventh century B.C. (Temple of Hera at Olympia), and are now to be found in all the lands adjacent to the Mediterranean. Han dynasty models suggest that this pattern may have evolved originally in China. Pantiles, in which the overlap is combined with the tile itself, are found in N.W. Europe including Scandinavia, Japan and Java, and plain flat tiles are used throughout Central Europe – including Britain – where there was previously a tendency to use wooden shingles.

At various times in Europe tiles have been used for floors; either small ones for mosaic designs, such as we find in the North of France, or large decorated ones, such as were made in many monastic potteries during the Middle Ages, of which the Chapter House in West-minster Abbey is a good example. Their resistance to abrasion, acids and other destructive agencies has recently made them popular in hospitals and scientific establishments where dust and porosity cannot be tolerated, and new systems have been devised for using large hollow-sectioned clay extrusions to lighten the weight of load-bearing upper floors in steel

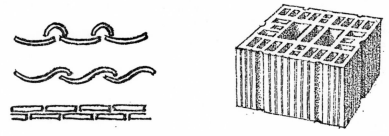

Traditional patterns of tiling and a modern hollow brick

and concrete constructions. These hollow floor blocks reduce considerably the amount of shuttering and supports required during erection, and the reinforced concrete beams, which ultimately give the floor its strength, are cast in preformed channels within them. Large extended hollow ceramic pieces are now being used for walls, and efforts are being made to perfect their manufacture in order to overcome the one disadvantage of bricks which is their small size and, consequently, rather slow rate of erection.

WATER SUPPLY AND SANITATION

Wherever large towns or cities have grown without adequate attention being given to water supply, sewage disposal and drainage the results have been the same: obnoxious smells, typhoid epidemics, cholera and, ultimately, large spreading fires which could not be fought, and it is curious to note how frequently this terrible situation has arisen in comparatively recent times in spite of the example set by most ancient civilizations. Far into the nineteenth century London was described as a 'Pest House of a Metropolis and Disgrace to the Nation' and repeated attempts to tackle the problem were met by the suggestion – even supported by *The Times* – that such epidemics were 'divine visitations which it would be impious to restrain'. In some quarters it was argued that 'it was expedient to keep the streets in their present state of filth in order to keep up the means of employing indigent persons as street sweepers and sweepers of crossings in removing it'. One of the arguments used on the side of the Sanitary Reformers of the time was to ask people to imagine the Emperor Constantine was visiting London and to contemplate his surprise at being told that public baths did not exist. There can be few towns left in the world today, however, that have not caught up in this respect with their counterparts thirty or forty centuries ago.

Water and sewage systems in the Indus Valley appear to have been complete and in advance of any other pre-classical race known to us. They included latrines with waste channels leading to cesspits and, in some cases, seated lavatories with sloping channels leading into pottery receptacles or brick drains. Both in the Indus Valley and in the

Middle East vertical drains have been found consisting of large bottomless pots resting one on top of another; those found at Ur measuring some 30 inches in diameter and being 5 feet high. The palace at Knossos in Crete provides another example of a complete system dating from over two thousand years B.C. Earthenware pipes found at Knossos are standard in size, 30 inches long and 6 inches wide, tapering to 4 inches to provide satisfactory interlock.

Greek and Roman pipes were also of standard dimensions with interlocking or socketed ends. By Roman times water supply must have been taken for granted, and the quantity consumed in Rome alone was comparable to that of the present day. At Rome's zenith there appear to have been about eight hundred bathing establishments within the city for which the supplies of water were borne by eleven aqueducts, three of which are still in use, and one of which, built in 146 B.C., was 58 miles long.

The decline of town life and civic organization for nearly seventeen hundred years after the Roman Empire is somewhat mystifying, though an accusing finger could perhaps be pointed at the established Christian churches which early on withdrew from contact with daily life, leaving a vacuum in moral leadership in which selfishness and lack of social conscience grew until it became necessary for governments to act by legislation. In 1842 a disturbing report on the 'Sanitary Conditions of the Labouring Population of Great Britain' was published by Edwin Chadwick, who has since become known as the 'Father of Sanitary Science', showing that although parts of London and a few other large towns were drained after a fashion, the majority had no sewers at all. House drainage was either non-existent or completely unsatisfactory. Renewed outbreaks of disease in the year of the Irish famine (1845) threatened to assume the proportions of another Black Death and eventually, in 1848, a General Board of Health was set up by the first Public Health Act. Vested interests attempted to extend the use of porous earthenware drainage pipes which had been used extensively in agriculture since the eighteenth century, but Edwin Chadwick eventually managed to convince all parties that impervious salt-glazed stoneware ones were the only solution.

The enormous demand likely to follow such a decision was foreseen by Henry Doulton, son of John Doulton who established the famous firm at Lambeth at the beginning of the nineteenth century, and in 1846, he established a new works near by devoted solely to the production of vitrified salt-glazed pipes. After initial technical difficulties had been overcome the demand for these pipes grew at such a pace that within three years factories were also opened at Dudley and St. Helens. The first town in Britain to install a salt-glazed sewer system meeting the approval of the new Board of Health was Alnwick in Northumberland. Such pipes and fittings are now so common that they are barely noticed and they serve many purposes, for instance, hundreds of miles of salt-glazed piping have been laid by the Post Office and Electricity Boards to act as protective conduits for cables. Non-porous stoneware material was soon used for all sanitary fittings and smooth, hygienic surfaces were created on the rough clay by coating them with fine white slip.

Most pipes in the early civilizations were thrown on the potter's wheel, though some were clearly made by wrapping clay round wooden formers. Hand-operated extruding machinery became available early in the nineteenth century for the production of agricultural drainage pipes two to three inches in diameter, and after the Great Exhibition of 1851 machinery for all types of ceramic operations, including clay preparation, improved rapidly. Concrete has been used for very large pipes since 1906.

Ancient thrown water pipes

It is generally considered that once salt-glazed pipes have been laid they may be forgotten, but unfortunately, though this may be true of the pipes, it is not always so of the joints. Over a long length some flexibility is required to allow for even minute earth movements and considerable research has been needed to produce cements which will allow for this.

FURNACES, REFRACTORIES AND FUELS

The earliest pottery in all parts of the world was simply burned in a bonfire, and as a method this has remained without improvement in primitive parts of Africa, Indonesia and India. In Europe, Asia Minor and the Near East kilns of upright shape were evolved in early times and remained in favour until very recently, and in the Far East long-shaped kilns inclined on a hillside had been evolved before the time of Christ. These upright and horizontal kilns were both capable of refinement and developed along similar paths.

The bonfire is wasteful of heat and severely limiting in the type of ware it will produce, but some skill is needed to burn large pots successfully. In most areas it appears that the fire is conducted on a bed of stones which may be pre-heated to warm the pots before they are subjected to the onslaught of the flames. The pots are skilfully piled on these stones with plenty of fuel between them and, before lighting, the whole heap is covered with sticks and faggots. As the wood burns away it is replaced by armfuls of grass or straw to prevent the ware from being suddenly chilled. The whole process is over within two or three hours and the highest temperature reached is not likely to be in excess of 900° C. The ware will always be porous and unglazed though the sandy clays used may acquire a pleasingly varied surface quality from the flames. The bricks of Mesopotamia and probably the Indus Valley were fired in a similar way, though the process was prolonged – perhaps by several weeks – by piling earth over the clay and fuel to form a clamp.

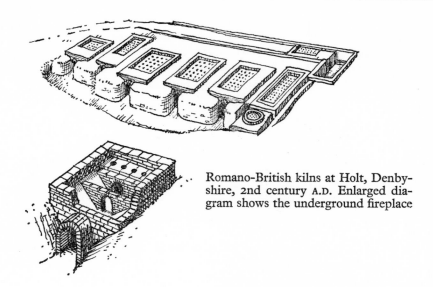

Romano-British kilns at Holt, Denby-
shire, 2nd century A.D. Enlarged dia-
gram shows the underground fireplace

The upright kilns of the Near East and Europe were initially simple structures in which the pots were contained in a chamber with a perforated floor, erected over a pit containing the fire. The flames played through the ware and left by a small hole in the roof which served also to create draught. With refinement of proportion and stoking methods temperatures of 1100° C. could be reached fairly easily, though much of the firing on these continents was conducted at temperatures considerably below this level. In most early structures of this type – including Roman examples – there was no door, the upper part of the chamber above ground level being rebuilt each time the kiln was loaded.

The Far Eastern kilns were generally of far greater size and were therefore fired less

Italian kiln with permanent chamber
for firing tin-glazed earthenware,
about 1550 A.D. From a contemporary
manuscript by Piccolpasso

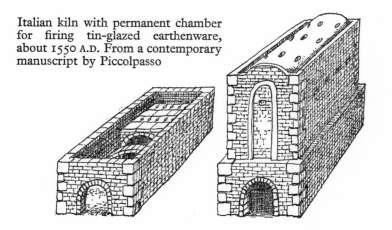

frequently. In the early days the kiln consisted of a long tunnel built partly above ground, with a large firemouth at the lower end, and smaller ones at intervals up the sides which were used to supplement the heating along the entire length. Draught was created without a chimney by the inclination of the kiln.

Left: English 14th century up-draught kiln, diameter about 7 feet. Pots were stacked on the platform as well as over the clay arches, and a new roof of wicker and clay was built for each firing

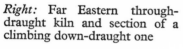

Right: Far Eastern through-draught kiln and section of a climbing down-draught one

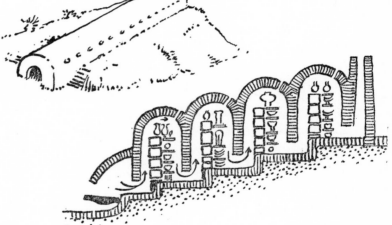

Both these through-draught or 'up-draught' kilns were restricted in their maximum temperatures by the ease with which the flames rushed through them, and it was not long before the Eastern kilns were broken down their length into a number of nearly separate chambers in which the flames were first of all forced to the top by meeting a baffle wall, and were then drawn down through the ware before going into the next chamber via an outlet at the bottom of the wall. Each separate chamber after the first – sometimes twenty or more – also received supplementary heat from fireplaces set in its sides. The same 'down-draught' principle was later applied to European upright kilns to great advantage by moving the fire to the side and building the kiln on ground level. After meeting the baffle wall in front of the fireplace – or fireplaces ranged at points round

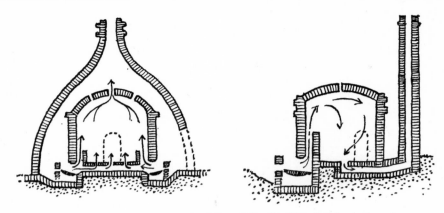

European up- and down-draught kilns. The familiar bottle or hovel serves
as a chimney

the side – the flames shot to the dome to be sucked down again through the centre of the
ware into several flue outlets underneath the floor, and thence to a separate chimney at
the side. The principle of the down-draught kiln ensures that the flame is kept within the
kiln for a longer period – it travels almost twice the distance inside – and therefore higher
temperatures are easily reached with only a fractional increase in the quantity of fuel
consumed.

The kilns mentioned so far are all of the intermittent type, that is to say they are packed
with ware whilst cold, and both the kiln and ware are heated together. It has been estimated
that European upright kilns require about 30 – 40 % of the fuel consumed to heat the
brickwork and another 10 – 12 % to heat the saggars in which the ware is protected from
the flames, and it is only to be expected that recent research should have been directed
towards eradicating at least some of this waste. The Oriental kilns were considerably more
efficient in this respect because the heat from one chamber contributed to the firing of
the next, so towards the end of a firing – ten days to a fortnight's work – the last chamber
or two required only a little extra heat from their side fire-boxes. Various solutions were
tried in Europe, notably the famous circular, or oval, Hoffmann brick kilns which consisted of at least fourteen chambers adjacent to one another, fired in order so that the heat
from a cooling chamber was used to preheat the next. A more recent solution has been the
development of tunnel ovens where the central spot of a kiln, perhaps three hundred feet
in overall length, is kept permanently at maximum temperature whilst the ware is slowly
moved towards it on trucks. The wheels of the trucks are well insulated against the heat,
and the heat from the ware that has already passed the hot zone is used to pre-heat the
air supply to the burning fuel – another great economy. In firing common building bricks
tunnel kilns have reduced fuel consumption from an average of $3\frac{1}{4}$ hundredweights of coal
per ton of bricks to $1\frac{1}{2}$ hundredweights per ton, a saving of over 50 %. Tunnel kilns were
first considered in France in 1751, but difficulties were encountered in their construction

which delayed common acceptance till after World War I, and they did not gain real acceptance in this country till after World War II.

Not surprisingly pottery kilns have always been built of clay, and natural limitations of temperature have been imposed on some races by the absence in their lands of what are known as 'refractory clays' capable of withstanding high temperatures. Refractory clays, or 'fireclays' are usually associated with coal deposits, and represent the earth on which the primeval forests fed for thousands of years denuding them of metallic salts which, if remaining in clays, cause them to melt at low temperatures (see pages 39 to 40, Chapter 2, and pages 118 to 119, Chapter 7). Fireclays can comfortably withstand temperatures up to 1500° C. without softening. Chinese potters knew of their existence in early times and their work developed with a freedom that was denied to their contemporaries in the Near East who, in other ways, were perhaps technically ahead of them. Early kilns were probably built with clay in much the same way as the larger pots and were baked at the same time as the first batch of ware, but more recently kilns have been built of pre-fired fireclay bricks so that shrinkage of the walls is eliminated.

Furnaces of all kinds have for long been lined with fireclay coatings or bricks, and it is true to say that any industry requiring heat above the dullest red glow could not carry on without this material. Some industries nowadays, however, work at temperatures in excess of that which can be withstood by ordinary fireclay and their specialized demands have been met by the admixture of other materials to fireclay, or the use of pure ceramic oxides.

The components of clay – silica and alumina – have complementary properties; on its own silica can withstand considerable temperatures, but, owing to its continually altering crystal structure under heat, it cannot cope with rapid and frequent rise and fall of temperature without shattering. The use of silica as a refractory material, or clays in which there is a preponderance of it, is therefore confined to situations where high temperatures are maintained for long periods, such as the roofs of open-hearth steel furnaces operating for months on end at temperatures around 1650° C. (Plate 3).

Alumina has a higher melting point than silica (2050° C. against 1730° C.) and does not suffer from expansion or contraction due to changes of crystal formation on heating or cooling. It is therefore more useful than silica as a refractory, though more expensive because the few deposits found in the world are in great demand as aluminium ore.

The use of isolated ceramic oxides as refractory materials has increased considerably in recent years, and silica and alumina have now been joined by lime, chrome and magnesia, each of which has properties that suit some circumstances better than others. Considerable care has to be taken in deciding which oxide or clay should be used to withstand any particular combination of temperature change, molten slag, chemical or abrasive action occurring in the heat zone where they will be employed.

The idea of using substances other than clays in ceramics, and the refractory requirements of rocket, jet or nuclear engines, have led to the development of materials such as silicon nitride, silicon carbide, boron nitride and others (Plate 8). These chemically constant materials can be machined like metals when cold or part fired, and, as they do not shrink in firing, they are capable of accepting a similar degree of accuracy of workmanship. Some technologists believe that such simple binary compounds will ultimately replace all the clay used by the ceramic industry, and that the vastly increased cost of raw materials could be saved time and again from the abandonment of the elaborate procedures involved in subjecting nature's clay to the standardization required by mass production methods.

The iron and steel industries of Britain use annually about $1\frac{1}{2}$ million tons of refractory brickwork for lining the blast furnaces in which the crude ore is reduced to metal, and the Bessemer, open-hearth or other furnaces in which the crude products of the blast furnaces are converted into steel. Iron was produced for many centuries all over the world in clay-lined pits using charcoal fuel, but the de-forestation of the areas concerned – in Britain; Kent, Sussex and the Forest of Dean – became so acute that from Elizabethan times onwards a search was made for other fuels. Outcrops of coal had been worked spasmodically in this country by the Romans and early in the seventeenth century attempts were made to use it to replace charcoal. Where heat alone was needed – as is the case with pottery – coal was immediately satisfactory, but iron, glass and brewing were affected chemically by the fuel so there was some delay in its general acceptance. Attempts were made in 1603 to purify coal in the way that charcoal is made from wood and some success was achieved by 1648 which led ultimately to the growth of the gas and coke industry.

The gas and coke industry is now another major consumer of refractory brickwork, using over $\frac{1}{4}$ of a million tons per year. Over the years this industry has increased its operating temperature; at first iron retorts were satisfactory, then later they were made of fireclay and now they are lined with almost pure silica bricks. This rise in operating temperature is typical of most industries; it throws into sharp focus the primary importance of the refractory branch of the ceramic industry which receives little publicity and is barely known to exist.

Another highly important branch of the ceramic industry is that concerned with the production of porcelain insulators for the electrical industry. The first of these was made around the middle of the nineteenth century – again by Doultons – and the rapid extension of electrical illumination as well as telegraphic communication after that date led to a demand for new and intricate shapes in quantity. It was discovered that these intricate shapes could be accurately pressed in steel moulds provided separating oil was added to the clay powder and not, as would be the usual practice, coated over the mould. The manufacture of the very large insulators for the modern grid system and for other high voltage layouts is now among the most skilled and spectacular branches of the industry, and, curiously, the work is all done by hand with the aid of the most primitive throwing tools – some wire, a sponge and a few pieces of wood and bent metal. Some of these insulators, fired in one piece, reach a height of 14 feet (Plate 9). Owing to the peculiar nature of the special porcelain clays employed it is possible to apply the glaze to these electrical wares without biscuit firing, and hence only one firing at 1300° C. is employed. Similar importance must be attached to the manufacture of sparking plugs for internal combustion engines, the first patent for which was taken out by H. K. Shank of Columbus, Ohio, in 1888.

Until the refractory and insulator branches of the ceramic industry had developed efficient wares and appliances for the gas, oil and electrical industries, the only fuels available for firing their own kilns were wood or coal. Now, however, there is a choice of town gas, producer gas, natural gas, oil or electricity, each of which has advantages or disadvantages of its own, but all of which are generally found to be better for industrial application than any of the solid fuels. In this country electricity is expensive, but this is not the case in other places where it is produced by hydro plants. It is a clean fuel which dispenses with any need for the protection of the ware in fireclay boxes or saggars, and is ideal for tunnel kilns, small experimental ones or those for the studio potter. All Wedgwood ware has been electrically fired since before the war.

The state of the atmosphere in Stoke-on-Trent – the centre of the British pottery industry – when over 600 small firms were firing two or three kilns a day with coal, each kiln consuming up to eight tons of fuel per day, is difficult to imagine. Photographs of the district at this time may sometimes be seen. The Clean Air Act has now done away with almost all solid fuel kilns to the benefit of the inhabitants, though one suspects that the gas- or oil-fired replacements still contaminate the atmosphere with invisible impurities!

UTENSILS

The earliest utensils were probably made from skins, fruits or rushes, and it cannot have been long before it was discovered that the interstices of baskets could be sealed with clay enabling them to contain grain or liquid without loss. Once the material had entered the kitchen it was discovered that it became hardened by fire, and that when burned it was no longer necessary for it to be held in shape by basketwork or any other support. Neither of these discoveries was difficult to make; they did not wait to be passed by word of mouth from tribe to tribe, or to be carried as trade secrets by bands of itinerant craftsmen, but were made spontaneously all over the world as soon as fire had been mastered and the hearth established as the focal centre of existence. The fact that this social evolution did not take place everywhere at the same pace has meant that the history of domestic pottery is complicated. Some tribes in Africa produce today a similar kind of pottery to that which was in use in Europe four thousand years ago, and quite double this length of time in countries round the Eastern shores of the Mediterranean.

As they were made by the same means to serve similar purposes the early pots of one tribe did not differ greatly from those of another, and the history of domestic pottery is further confused by the absence of the dramatic changes of form that are seen in, for instance, means of transport or even the cooking stove itself. The fundamental jar, bowl and platter shapes remain as useful today as when they were first evolved. Subtle changes of social custom have created the need for a profusion of sizes of the fundamental forms of clay wares, and slight modifications have been made in terms of additional handles, spouts or lids. The call for smoother, lighter and more hygienic wares has been met by alteration to the raw materials in contrast to some crafts where the material is always constant and there has been continuous development of tools and techniques. The introduction of the wheel some four thousand years ago is the only major change of technique to affect pottery craft until the industrialization of the nineteenth century, and even such improvements already noted in the construction of pottery kilns have been thought of as much in terms of economy of fuel as in improvements to the ware.

The greatest single improvement to the fabric of pots has been the sealing of clay by a covering of glaze which not only made pots hygienic, but also made possible the use of a wide range of beautiful surface texture, or colour, to which pattern could be freely applied. Such pattern is for ever subject to fashion and racial preference, so that we see considerable variety of artistic expression as we look around the world from Europe to the Far East and America. This aspect of pottery history is interesting, but in these few pages there is room to discuss only the development of the pottery materials and techniques which are used in schools and studios today. Information about decoration will be found in most of the books listed in the bibliography.

The discovery of glass and glaze is quite a different matter to the spontaneous discovery of burning clay, and is an event which could only have happened in a few areas of the world because it is unlikely that all the ingredients involved would often be put together by accident. The first discovery of glass seems to have been made before 4000 B.C., though it was not allied to clay as a glaze coat until much later, nor were methods discovered by which the material could be shaped into useful forms for quite another two thousand five hundred years; it was enjoyed for its own sake in the form of beads and ornaments in the manner of precious stones. These discoveries appear to have been made in Egypt where the sands contain salts of sodium carbonate and where quartz, malachite, steatite and limestone are readily available. It has been suggested that the first evidence of the material may have been discovered when some malachite, which was frequently used as a grinding material or, when ground, as green eye shadow, was accidentally heated with some soda washing agent. Quartz and malachite were frequently carved and their surfaces coated with glass mixtures which were fired on to give an exquisite range of blues, greens and turquoises. Quartz was also crushed and mixed to a plastic paste with soda and organic matter so that it could be moulded, or even thrown, producing brightly coloured jewellery, vessels and figurines known as 'Egyptian faience'.

Egyptian faience hippopotamus

Glass and glazed ceramics developed alongside one another in Near Eastern lands. Glass objects were moulded over cores of sand contained within cloth bags in both Egypt and Mesopotamia from 1500 B.C. onwards, and the first attempts were made at blowing the material into hollow forms early in the Christian era. The techniques were perfected by Roman times and as the Mediterranean lands were conquered conditions became such that itinerant craftsmen could move freely into other lands. They were working North of the Alps by A.D. 50 and at least three works were established in Britain at Colchester, Warrington and Caistor. The extent of the technical accomplishment achieved in these times can be gauged from the discovery of blown glass window panes in Pompeii measuring 21 inches by 28, and a cast sheet measuring 40 inches by 28 of $\frac{1}{2}$ inch thickness.

Doubtless the idea of using plastic clay as a support for coloured glass grew from the Egyptian 'faience' technique, though the early glasses containing much soda and potash did not adhere to the clay too well. In Mesopotamia these 'alkaline' glazes were soon joined by a lead-based material better suited to the clay, recipes for which are recorded on tablets from Babylon dated as early as 1700 B.C. Once perfected lead glazes spread from Mesopotamia to the Far East, and the recipes remained almost unaltered in Europe and the North Mediterranean lands throughout Roman times until quite recently.

Rich honey-coloured, green, or blue lead glazes were used for a long time by the great Han and T'ang dynasty potters of China, but their use declined as white stoneware and porcelain bodies evolved and firing temperatures increased.

The evolution of porcelain is a typical result of the almost universal desire for refinement in domestic and decorative ceramics, and success in this field came in China at the time when Europe was barely recovering from the collapse of the Roman Empire. The success was no doubt due in part to the availability of suitable clays and glaze materials, but evidence of persistent research by trial and error can be seen from much ware of the Han and T'ang dynasties. Potters of the Sung dynasty lifted the craft above almost every other art and porcelain was regarded by emperors and kings alike as being more beautiful than precious stones. The subtle colouring, delicate form and warm feel of the surface of this ware affected almost the whole subsequent history of the craft the world over. Porcelain reached Persia and other Near Eastern countries by overland trade route before the turn of the first millennium A.D., and set on foot a process of refinement of the local wares in imitation. The impact of quantities of later translucent porcelain transported by sea in the sixteenth and seventeenth centuries to Western Europe (Plate 42) was enough to very nearly ruin our own industries which were still producing brown lead glazed wares from red earthenware clays covered with black and white applied decorations (see frontispiece).

Geologically the Near East and Europe were at a distinct disadvantage. The materials available to all the potters of the Near East were grey or whitish sandy clays and the crude material for glaze making which had been used originally. The Chinese clays and porcelain bodies were fine and highly plastic so that a delicacy and variety of form became a characteristic of their ware matching the subtle greens, reds and varied rich blacks of their glazes produced from felspars and ashes. The Near Eastern clay was not even plastic enough to be thrown without the addition of some sticky organic matter to keep it together, but yet the potters were able to produce wares of rugged beauty, and, because of their lower working temperatures, to use a range of colour which made up in brilliance for what it lacked in subtlety. There was little they could do to improve their clay, but whiter glazes were soon produced incorporating tin oxide, and an exquisite range of metallic lustres produced by alterations to the customary firing techniques for lead glazes in which a clean smokeless atmosphere was usually considered essential.

The techniques of tin-glazing and lustre gradually spread from Persia to Europe after A.D. 1100. Spain was conquered by Moorish races soon after the turn of the century and factories were established which had produced superb lustre wares before another century had passed. Production of lustre ware has continued until today, but there has been a steady decline of aesthetic merit since the fifteenth or sixteenth centuries.

The Moors also established tin-glazed pottery on the island of Majorca and by A.D. 1400 we find this type of ware being made with exquisite quality by the Renaissance potters in Italy. By A.D. 1500 the technique had spread to France and Holland, and somewhat later was taken up in Britain at Liverpool, Bristol (Plate 41) and Lambeth. Various names are used for these tin-glazed wares painted in soft blues, greens, yellows, purples and browns. The word 'faience' should be reserved for work produced at Faenza, 'delft' for the Dutch variety and 'maiolica' for that produced in Majorca. (Egyptian 'faience' is a misnomer which has been unfortunately adopted universally.)

The European public of A.D. 1650 could make their choice from three radically different types of pottery which represent the main streams of the craft. By this time the heyday of Sung pottery was over and the succeeding potters of the Ming dynasty concentrated on plain white porcelain, finely painted with scenes or patterns in blue, which was exported in quantity by the East India Company (Plate 42). Beside this refined, translucent ware the blue and white or coloured tin-glazed wares available locally looked decidedly crude, and the third choice – the peasant red clay wares decorated with black and white clay and casually coated with thick honey-coloured transparent lead glaze – looked worse still. It is understandable that at this time the wealthy should fall for the Oriental porcelain, but with our more distant view of the scene we can appreciate the merits of the other kinds of pottery and realize that it is pointless to compare them. They must each be considered in the light of their antecedents and enjoyed for their own sake. Tin-glazed ware has a warm unsophisticated quality which is often emphasized by the light note of the freely painted decoration, and the red clay peasant ware, known as 'slipware' after the manner of its decoration, is bold, often very decorative, and glowing with rich earthy colour.

However, in A.D. 1650 the choice of the wealthy classes in Europe was all-important and a frantic search was made for white clays which could yield a ware of equivalent brilliance to the Eastern porcelain. There are many stories connected with this search and the history of pottery written for the lay public often devotes considerable space to the subject. The clays were in fact available in Germany, Austria, France and Britain and were quickly

1. Babylon; a typical scene of the considerable remains left by the early brick-building civilizations

2. Steel, concrete, glass and bricks—the raw materials of modern building—are all produced in high temperature, clay lined, furnaces, and involve reactions between fluxes, alumina and silica at some stage of their manufacture

3. Refractory lined annealing oven in a steelworks

4. A glassblower drawing molten material from a refractory pot set in a furnace

5. High powered rectifier; one of the many applications of ceramics in electronics, radio and telecommunications

6, 7. Ceramics in the chemical industry: *above*, an acid production plant. *Right*, a filter tank 5 ft. by 4 ft. by 3 ft. 6 in. deep

8. Experimental refractories; silicon carbide (black), silicon nitride (grey) and boron nitride (white)

9, 10. Large scale industrial ceramics; *left*, making a porcelain bush insulator; *above*; an acid storage jar

11. Two halves of the same brick, that on the left having been almost glassified by an excessive temperature for the clay

12. Clay finally turned into glass after it had melted sufficiently to flow inside the coils of a kiln element

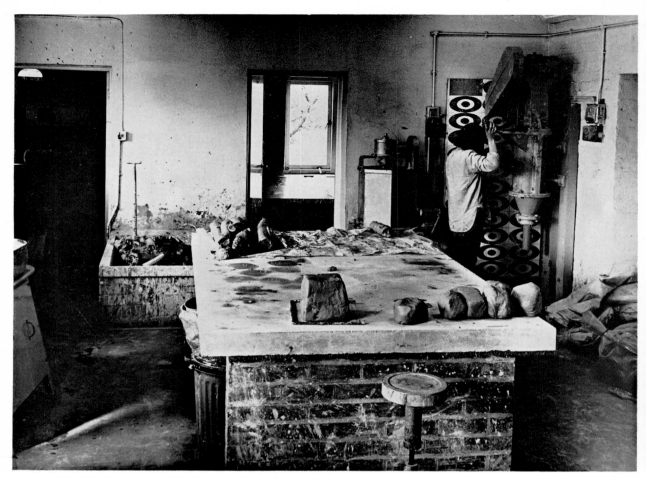

13. Equipment suitable for a medium sized pottery. Scrap clay is put in the dustbins behind the wheel on the left; the scraps are dried in the concrete trough against the end wall (two tubular electric heaters underneath) and, when ready, are fed, together with some new clay, through the vertical pugmill in the corner. The pugged clay is stored in brick built bins visible through the centre doorway. The smaller machine is a blunger for stirring clay scraps into a slip which can be sieved before being dried out in the trough. The concrete bench in the foreground is an essential; in this case provision is made to take dustbins of sand, grog and dry powdered clay underneath. The door on the left leads to a damp room for the storage of uncompleted pots

14. The down-draught kiln, described in Chapter 5, under construction. In this case new bricks were used only in the interior

15. The completed kiln being fired

16

17

18

19

16, 18, 19. Pots and sculpture made from jointed sheets of clay
17. Large twig vase made by wrapping a sheet of clay round a baulk of timber.
20, 21, 22. Coiled pots. 20, partly made on a wheel. 21, a stool built upside down over a large dish mould. 22, un-smoothed coils coated with a dark slip and scraped when dry

20

21

22

23. The simplification of form resulting from hollow building techniques

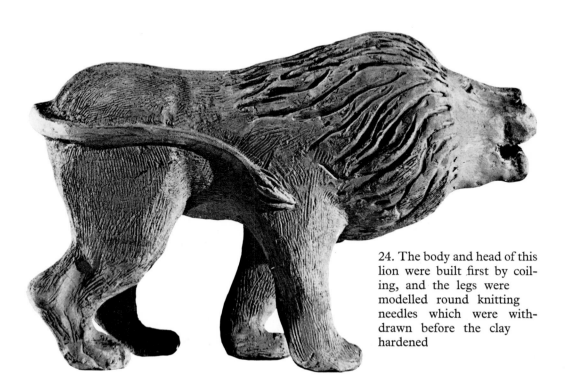

24. The body and head of this lion were built first by coiling, and the legs were modelled round knitting needles which were withdrawn before the clay hardened

25, 26. The ancient technique of direct modelling from rolls and sheets used by a child (*left*) and a professional potter (*right*)

27. Lion made hollow by simple pinching methods

28, 29. The designs on these two tiles were engraved and filled with white slip which was scraped off the surface when nearly dry

30, 31. The effectiveness of these two relief designs is due partly to the fact that the modelling is sometimes higher and sometimes lower than the original surface which has almost ceased to exist

32, 33. Examples of unguided work by young children. *Above*, (32) a crocodile leaps over a bridge. *Right*, (33) an engine formed by the inventive use of a sheet of clay and an apple corer

34. Teapot formed from a thumbed bowl by a very young child. Adult help was sought to make the spout hollow

35, 36. *Left* (35), Moulded dish decorated by drawing freely into soft clay with a blunt point. *Right* (36), Cheeseboard decorated by cutting with a loop of spring steel. Both designs were brushed with oxides which were scraped off the surface when the clay had dried

37. Stoneware dish made from the mould illustrated on page 108

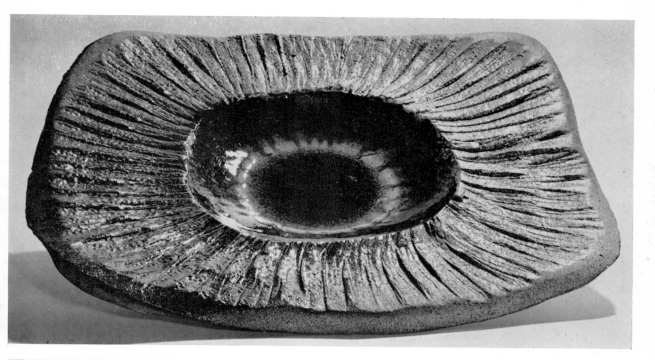

38. Large dish moulded by pressing a sheet of coarse clay into the spare wheel cover of an old car. Borax frit was heaped in the centre to form a pool of glass over a coat of iron oxide

39. Exquisite interpretation of the forms of chessmen in terms of rolled and pinched clay. Colour contrast was obtained by mixing red clay into the light coloured coarse body

40, 41. The last of European pre-industrial pottery. The charming tin glazed wares (40) tried to hold their market by imitating the designs of Oriental porcelain, but, after this final superb flourish (41) the slipwares were relegated to the kitchen

42. Oriental porcelain; the ware that changed the whole of European pottery after the 17th century. This cargo, however, was lost in transit

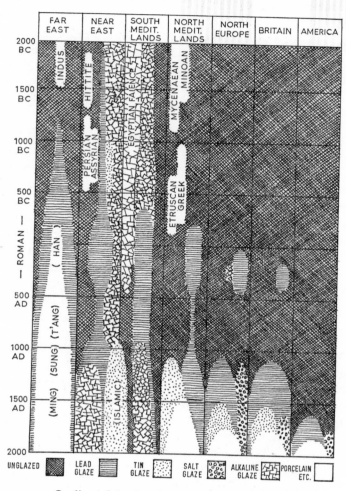

	FAR EAST	NEAR EAST	SOUTH MEDIT. LANDS	NORTH MEDIT. LANDS	NORTH EUROPE	BRITAIN	AMERICA

Outline of the development of pottery glazes

unearthed – they had already been used for powdering wigs – and soon after A.D. 1700 various types of European porcelain appeared from factories at St. Cloud, Limoges, Meissen, Vienna and Berlin and Britain. One of the most commercially successful answers to the fashion for whitewares was made by the Staffordshire potters who evolved a workable white earthenware clay which, when fired at a moderately high temperature (1180° C.), produced quality ware at only a fraction of the cost of porcelain. White earthenware of a kind was introduced by Astbury in 1725 and improved, after many experiments, by Josiah Wedgwood in 1760. It has remained the staple product of Stoke-on-Trent ever since and is what we all use for everyday tableware.

5

In A.D. 1800 Spode produced a quite revolutionary whiteware which was considerably smoother and whiter than even the Oriental porcelain. The body of this ware contained up to 40% of animal bone ash and it is interesting to note the reference in its name – bone china – to the competition with the Orient. Because it is coated with only a relatively low temperature glaze, bone china can be satisfactorily decorated with a wide range of enamel colours applied by printing or by hand. Bone china proved immediately to be the answer to any Oriental ware and has won its place in markets all over the world; it is now produced by many important firms in Stoke.

Europe produced one type of high-fired coarse pottery which stands quite alone in the history of ceramics, and which has, as was mentioned in the section on water supply, proved most beneficial to our society. This is the salt-glazed stoneware evolved in the Rhinelands during the twelfth and thirteenth centuries. No other pottery is produced in the same way as this, which is glazed by throwing common salt into the kiln when it is nearly white hot, and it is difficult to imagine how the process was discovered in the first place. The roughly mottled glaze which we see everywhere on drainpipes and fittings is admirably suited to embossed decoration, and motifs can be painted in strong blue colour when a light grey firing clay is used producing the familiar German beer mugs and jugs. This process was adopted at Fulham in the seventeenth century and a form of white salt-glazed ware was ultimately produced which was successful for a time.

In the earliest days pottery was a family business with each man being skilled in all the processes. The wheel was slowly introduced from 2500 B.C. onwards, and it is always said that as each tribe or race evolved a satisfactory system of throwing the men took over the craft from the women who had carried the burden of clay preparation and potmaking by hand as an added chore. Doubtless the introduction of wheel-throwing brought in an element of team work, and the faster production rate would mean that one workshop could meet the needs of a large community instead of each smaller unit troubling to meet their own.

The introduction of the factory system into ceramics, in which each workman is skilled in only one process, can possibly be attributed to Josiah Wedgwood to whom the Stoke industry is indebted in many ways. Wedgwood, born in A.D. 1730, wished to be a thrower, but he was crippled by an attack of smallpox in his early youth and, though he reached a degree of competence in the craft (his wheel is on exhibition at Hanley Museum), he could not achieve his ambition. However, his energies turned into other channels; in 1759, feeling that the pottery industry of Stoke was in decline, he commenced a long series of experiments to improve the quality of clay body, glaze and form of the staple earthenware products. Within ten years these experiments had proved so fruitful that he was able to build for himself a large, efficiently planned factory, surrounded by a village of model dwellings for his workpeople, which he called Etruria to signify a renaissance of the art of the potter. Wedgwood's work is now renowned, and the firm he founded has continued to set an example to every industry in terms of factory organization, quality control and consideration shown to its employees.

From 1800 onwards the family pottery businesses began to decline, and the factory system with highly skilled, specialized operatives became increasingly common throughout the world, developing a new type of ware which is inimitable by the studio craftsman doing all his own processes. Under factory conditions it is inevitable that the ware acquires the stamp of the machine and becomes dehumanized. For several generations designers lost all contact with the craft for which they were designing and their business descended to one of pattern inventing and flower painting, but when the products had descended to the lowest possible ebb in the 1930's it became imperative that something was done. The problems of producing pleasing wares by machine are not confined to the pottery industry and it has been solved only by returning to the beginning; that is by training designers in a manner which leads them *to discover for themselves* the ways by which their materials can be fashioned and decorated, almost as though they were themselves born in a cave. This process of discovery starts long before a child is of school age.

Bibliography to Chapter 3

Technological Histories

C. Singer, E. J. Holmyard, A. R. Hall and T. J. Williams (joint editors) A HISTORY OF TECHNOLOGY. *5 vols. Oxford Press 1957*. Fascinating reading on every subject; excellent clear line drawings and indexes of names and subjects. Far too expensive (over £40) for the individual, but standard reference material that no library could possibly afford to be without.

Norman Davey, A HISTORY OF BUILDING MATERIALS. *Phoenix House 1961*. The author has been working for many years at the Government Building Research Station, Watford. The book presents full and authoritative information in a manner that is of interest to specialist or non-specialist alike. Illustrated with drawings and photographs, and containing detailed bibliographies.

Alec Clifton-Taylor, THE PATTERN OF ENGLISH BUILDING. *Batsford 1962*. The sections on bricks, tiles, unburnt earth and glass contain much fascinating material relevant to this chapter, but the rest of the book will also be enjoyed. The information on the geology of these islands could prove useful to the potter.

Lane Mitchell, CERAMICS, STONE AGE TO SPACE AGE. *McGraw-Hill 1963*. A brief account written for American schoolchildren covering in general terms the whole of modern ceramic technology. Such information is not readily available elsewhere.

The History of Pottery

The early history of pottery falls within the realm of archaeology about which a spate of elaborate, well illustrated and expensive publications has recently appeared. The publishers Thames & Hudson have led the way in both expensive and paperback productions, and readers are referred to their current lists. Specially recommended are THE DAWN OF CIVILIZATION and the series of paperbacks – THE LIBRARY OF EARLY CIVILIZATIONS – which have evolved from its separate chapters. See also Thames & Hudson's sumptuous series THE STANDARD LIBRARY OF ANCIENT AND CLASSICAL ART (THE HITTITES, CRETE AND MYCENAE and the ART OF MESOPOTAMIA), the cheaper ANCIENT PEOPLES AND PLACES series – some of which are available as paperbacks – and various other volumes listed under the general heading of Art History.

Accumulated knowledge of ancient history is now so vast that one or two guide-books for the layman are useful. Leonard Cottrell has been especially helpful in this way and several of his books – THE LOST PHARAOHS, LOST CITIES and THE BULL OF MINOS – are available in Pan paperbacks. The stories of ancient races in America, Asia, Europe, the Middle East and India are brought vividly to life in one volume; Ivar Lissner, THE LIVING PAST, *Jonathan Cape 1957*, or *Illustrated Penguin 1965*.

The following volumes would serve well as general introductions to the history of pottery:

J. H. Eppens, POTTERY. *Merlin Press 1964*. A slender volume, part history and part manual, with excellent illustrations including some in colour.

R. G. Haggar, POTTERY THROUGH THE AGES. *Methuen 1959*. A concise account of the entire field illustrated throughout with pleasing drawings and maps (the latter especially welcome) by the author.

Bernard Rackham, A KEY TO POTTERY AND GLASS. *Blackie 1947*. To have the two histories side by side is useful. The author was for many years Keeper of the Department of Ceramics at the Victoria and Albert Museum, and his other writings include – long out of print – a standard reference work on English Pottery.

W. B. Honey, THE ART OF THE POTTER. *Faber and Faber 1944*. This book stands a little apart from the others in that it is not a chronological history, but an appreciation of the various historical phases of pottery production grouped under such headings as 'Form', 'Incised Slip and Other Decoration in Clay' and 'Painting'. The text is largely written around two hundred illustrations forming a representative selection of masterpieces from all periods. The author was until his death Keeper of the Department of Ceramics of the Victoria and Albert Museum and his published works include also standard reference books no ENGLISH POTTERY AND PORCELAIN (*A. and C. Black 1947*), THE CERAMIC ART OF CHINA AND OTHER COUNTRIES OF THE FAR EAST (*Faber and Faber 1945*) and EUROPEAN CERAMIC ART (*Faber and Faber 1952*).

George Savage, POTTERY THROUGH THE AGES. *Pelican 1959*. PORCELAIN THROUGH THE

AGES. *Pelican 1954.* Two inexpensive but comprehensive studies biased slightly towards the interests of the collector. Each contains 64 pages of plates.

Alison Kelly, THE STORY OF WEDGWOOD. *Faber 1962.* A brief account of the life and work of the great Josiah Wedgwood, and the history of the firm up to the present day.

THE FABER AND FABER MONOGRAPHS ON POTTERY AND PORCELAIN cover nearly all the periods of pottery history in detail and with copious illustrations.

Other books of interest, especially for the excellence of their illustrations are:

Griselda Lewis, A PICTURE HISTORY OF ENGLISH POTTERY. *Hulton Press 1956.*

Mario Prodan, THE ART OF THE T'ANG POTTER. *Thames & Hudson 1960.*

Hugo Munsterberg, CERAMIC ART OF JAPAN. *Charles E. Tuttle Co. 1964.*

Anthony du Boulay, CHINESE PORCELAIN. *Weidenfeld and Nicolson 1963.*

Fujio Koyana and John Figgess. TWO THOUSAND YEARS OF ORIENTAL CERAMICS. *Thames & Hudson 1961.*

Henry Lehmann, PRE-COLUMBIAN CERAMICS. *Elek Books 1962.*

Figure of a girl. Japan, Haniwa, 300–600 A.D.

Small solid models. Mayan warrior and goddess from Mohenjo-Daro

PART THREE

Chapter 4

Clay

Over the world there are many different kinds of clay, and the studio potter or teacher can derive much pleasure from exploring their various colours, textures and firing qualities. Those suggested in the list of materials at the end of the book represent but a few of the many good clays and bodies which can be obtained ready for use from merchants in Britain; it is interesting to try others, in particular any sold by merchants, brickworks or other pottery manufacturers in one's own district.

Potters soon learn to select suitable clays for the character of the work in hand, and for all its multifarious products, the ceramic industry as a whole uses quite a variety. Suppliers' catalogues also include some which are not intended to be used on their own, but which are blended into mixtures such as those used in the mass production of white earthenware or bone china tableware. However, before going on to discuss the uses of different clays it may be useful to digress on the way in which clay appeared on the Earth in the first place.

The descent of clay from granite was mentioned in Chapter 2, but it is more accurate to say that clay is generally descended from one of the three different minerals of which granite is composed. There was once more granite about the Earth than there is now, but because it is composed of large crystals much of it has been destroyed by the action of ice flows, alternate freezing and thawing and hot acidic solutions rising from inside the Earth. The whitish crystals in the rock are quartz which, when freed and finely crushed by ice or movement in water, become sand. The sparkling crystals are mica and the others, grey or pink, are crystals of felspar which can be broken down into clay and other substances.

It is thought that granite magma erupted in large quantities inserting itself as a blister between the basaltic rocks of the crust and layers of sedimentary rocks, such as limestone, which were already formed upon it. The overburden of sedimentary rock acted as an insulating layer causing the molten granite to cool slowly and form large crystals. The sedimentary layer also prevented the escape of vaporized acid solutions which arrived with the granite magma causing them to collect at high points where they attacked the hot felspar.* Clay deposits several hundred feet deep were formed at these peaks, and, within a geologically short space of time, the overburden of sedimentary rock was removed by wind, rain or ice. The exposed clay was soon spread over the surrounding district by the same agencies, though some deposits in the world have been left undisturbed.

KINDS OF CLAY

The original clay material is known as PRIMARY CLAY though the names CHINA CLAY or KAOLIN have come to be used from association with bone china manufacture or Oriental porcelain. Primary clay does not possess the attractive plastic quality associated with clay and it forms only part of a mixture, or BODY as mixtures are called in the industry. Most deposits are reasonably pure and china clay is easily separated by flotation from the unaltered sand or mica particles which form more than half the bulk of the raw mineral. The material has uses outside the pottery industry – about three-quarters of the amount quarried each year is used in papermaking or as a filler in linoleum and cheap cottons – and, as its chemical constituents are basic glaze ingredients, it is often found listed among the chemicals in a pottery supplier's catalogue rather than among the clays.

The plasticity of clay is induced by the grinding action of water and ice and is a quality that is to be found in the vast majority of clay deposits which have long since been moved away from their original sites of formation. These clays are broadly labelled SECONDARY CLAYS, but the name is rarely used because of the variety of them. On the journeys from the sites of formation they became mixed with varying proportions of other minerals in the Earth's crust, and names have been devised which give some indication of the kind or quantity of additional matter contained in them. The most frequent impurities are the remains of the decayed granite or felspar – lime, sand or potash – now no longer chemically combined with the clay, but the all-pervading oxide of iron has crept into most secondary clays in some quantity.

BALL CLAYS are secondary ones which have been moved from their sources and finely ground on their journey, but which have not acquired much iron oxide and therefore provide useful white or cream burning clays. The name 'ball clay' comes from an old system of transporting the material from the pits as round lumps in horses' saddlebags. In their raw state they are often stained grey, blue, or nearly black by decayed vegetable matter and, though this colour burns away entirely during the firing, it may be used to describe the clay in a merchant's price list. Among all clays perhaps the ball clays are the

* This chemical process can be outlined in the following equation:—

$$K_2O . Al_2O_3 . 6SiO_2 \;+\; x\; HCO_3 \;=\; Al_2O_3 . 2SiO_2 . 2H_2O \;+\; x\; K_2CO_3 \;+\; 4\;SiO_2$$

Felspar	Carbonic acid	Clay	Potassium carbonate	Silica (quartz or sand)

most plastic, so much so in fact that plasticity itself becomes a drawback in that it can cause too much shrinkage and warping. The WHITE, CREAM OR IVORY EARTHENWARE BODIES of industry are mixtures of over-plastic ball clay and under-plastic china clay with other additions of flint and felspar which increase fusibility. Neither these bodies nor the ball clays are especially suited to hand working except for occasional use as decorative coatings.

The pleasantest clays to use by hand, and those which are recommended for school or studio use, are the red or grey ones which are not quite so fine. These clays are also the commonest, acquiring their colour from vegetable matter and red or black iron oxide. RED CLAY – sometimes referred to as TERRACOTTA CLAY – may contain as much as 8% of iron oxide with other additions as well, but there is considerable variation. The additions have the effect of lowering the melting point; primary or china clay may begin to melt at about 1800° C., but some impure clays will be liquid at just over half this temperature. Red clays sold by reputable suppliers do not melt much below 1300° C.

Grey clays are called BUFF CLAYS in some price lists because they fire to this colour. They contain between 2% and 4% of iron oxide which, together with other additions, gives a melting point above 1400° C. enabling them to be used for stoneware fired between 1250° C. and 1350° C.

Additions of sand or other materials are often made to the buff clays in order to reduce shrinkage or cracking, and the mixtures, sold as STONEWARE BODIES, are strongly recommended. Sometimes an addition is made in the form of GROG which is clay that has already been fired and then finely ground. St. Thomas's Body mentioned earlier, and sold by Potclays Ltd., is a particularly good stoneware body; so too is Podmore's B.34.

The heat resistant FIRECLAYS mentioned in the previous chapter are usually grey in colour in their raw state and are sold by pottery suppliers or builders' merchants in powder form. In common with most other clays they develop their most interesting qualities when fired to a very high temperature, and their good working properties may be a little offset by their dull appearance when fired only to earthenware heat (1100° C.).

The shelves on which pots are supported in kilns are known as cranks in the industry and Potclays Ltd. sell a coarse fireclay and grog mixture, from which they could be made, under the name of CRANK MIXTURE. This prepared plastic refractory is most useful because its coarse, open texture allows it to be used freely for large, thick or irregular forms which would only crack if made from finer grained material. Crank Mixture is also a splendid additive to red or grey clays which seem too smooth for modelling purposes, or which seem too ready to crack on drying.

Many price lists include MODELLING CLAYS but it must be remembered that these are usually bodies of the white or cream earthenware type suited to the production of fine, lathe-turned models of teapots, tureens, etc., in preparation for the making of plaster moulds for mass production methods, and would be out of key with the bold, imaginative modelling of children, or the hand-thrown ware from a studio.

A pleasing variety of coarse bodies especially suitable for children's models and for firing in primitive kilns can also be made by weighing out proportions of powdered clays and soaking them, though there is a lot of labour attached to their final preparation which makes them difficult for general use. The following mixtures of both powdered and plastic clays are recommended:

	Powdered ingredients			Plastic ingredients				
Fireclay	2	1	4					
Pre-fired Fireclay Powder or Grog	1	1	4					
China Clay		1						
Red Clay			3	1	1		1	1
Crank Mixture				3	1	1	2	1
Grey or Buff Clay						1	2	1

Most clays are available in either powder or plastic forms. It may appear cheaper to buy powdered clay and add water, but, because of the fuel used in drying, this is not always so. Powdered clays are, however, useful for mixing decorative slips and they can be bought in small quantities for this purpose. Occasionally clay is sold in 'lump' form, but this has to be finely powdered before it can be soaked and prepared for use.

Prices range between fifteen and thirty shillings per hundredweight, and it is worth noting that the cost of transporting this quantity over the length of England is about the same. Fortunately Stoke-on-Trent, where most of the suppliers have their depots, is fairly central in England and this heavy transport rate reduces for larger quantities.

Local brickworks or potteries are often prepared to sell clay at a cheaper rate, and there are many deposits all over the world which may be dug for nothing with considerable enhancement of the sense of personal achievement and educational value. However, these clays rarely have the same quality – even after cleaning (see page 78) – as those provided by industrial suppliers, and they should be tested before much energy is expended with the spade. Some of them are inclined to melt suddenly at quite low temperatures. Taking into account the labour involved in preparing local clays, and the fact that they are likely to be inaccessible for so much of the year, it seems inevitable that most of the clay used in schools or studios will be bought ready for use.

KEEPING CLAY IN CONDITION

The condition of the clay is a factor of primary importance in any pottery studio and, though different conditions are required for different processes (see table on page 104), nothing much can be achieved without ample quantities of good plastic material being available. If the clay is a little too hard or too soft students quickly become disheartened, and in the average class there is little time to spare for correcting the condition. If it is only a little too soft models will not stand up and dishes will split; if it is a little too hard the clay cannot be shaped without cracking. Somewhere between these two lies a condition in which clay is attractive to use, it is soft but firm enough to remain in whatever position it is placed, and it coats the fingers with only the lightest film. No one can resist it.

Clay dries quickly in a warm atmosphere and, when hard, it cannot be worked soft again like plasticine. The reconditioning of a quantity which has been allowed to become dry is an arduous and messy job which has to be avoided at all costs by a disciplined system of working and storage. In an airtight container clay will keep moist for ever and actually improve a little in working qualities as its moisture content is distributed throughout even the minutest pores by capillary action. However, few containers are really airtight and provision must be made to keep the circulating current damp by standing the clay on a duckboard over an inch or two of water. Wet sacking and then polythene should be put on top of the clay beneath the lid. Dustbins are frequently used as clay stores but their round shape is inconvenient; an old water cistern, with a zinc or plastic lined wooden lid, is capable of holding two or three times as much for only little extra floor space and is easier to load or unload.

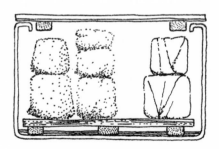

Water cistern adapted as a clay store

New clay should be in perfect condition when it arrives and will be wrapped in polythene sheeting (or bags which can be cut carefully to provide useful large sheets) as well as paper or sacking. If these wrappings are not damaged it will store well in a cool place as it is, but hundredweight lots are awkward to handle and difficult to unwrap whilst eager students are waiting. It is suggested that new clay is opened immediately it arrives and each hundredweight is cut into six or eight smaller pieces which are banged into cubes before being stacked neatly away in the clay store.

One successful and labour-saving method of dealing with clay in school classes is to distribute a few of these cubes at convenient points around the room and for the children to cut off cleanly with a wire as much as they need. The blocks must be kept under a damp cloth throughout the lesson and, though the children should be encouraged to feel free to poke and pummel the clay in front of them as much as they want, it should be clearly understood that the stock pieces are left alone. At the end of the lesson the clay remaining in good plastic condition is banged into new cubes before being returned to the store. The smaller pieces littering the benches and the discarded models will inevitably be a little dry; they should also be banged into cubes and either wrapped tightly in wet cloths or, if they feel very stiff, they should be pierced with several deep holes which are filled with water before wrapping in wet cloths or polythene. After a day or two this water will have permeated the block to some extent and a few moments of kneading will rework it into excellent condition. Provided the children do not feel restricted in the quantity they may use they will appreciate the efficiency of a method of this kind, and will acquire some respect for raw materials. The method is equally effective in studios.

Kneading and wedging are essential preparatory processes for most clay work and the knack associated with each has to be grasped so that they can be carried out with the minimum expenditure of energy. Kneading is precisely the same as the process used in bread-making and is the fastest possible method of evenly mixing clays of different colour. It is done (in small quantities at any rate) on a table of convenient height with an absorbent surface to which clay does not stick unless it is too wet (plaster, concrete, slate or paving

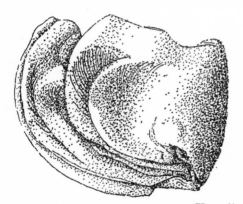 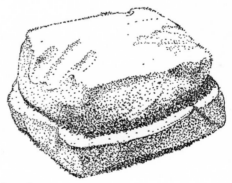

Kneading and wedging clay

stone). The soft clay lump is grasped on top by both hands which are then pushed into it by a thrust of the body. The hands are immediately moved back to the top and the movement is repeated until the clay has been folded over upon itself time and time again. With correct body movements a rhythm develops which makes comparatively light work of the job – those who rely on arm movements alone will soon tire – and if the hands are placed a little towards the top corners the clay preserves a tidy, manageable shape such as is illustrated. Clay which is a little too soft for use can be stiffened in a few seconds by kneading on thoroughly dry plaster and a slab should be made for the purpose.

Wedging fulfills a different function though it does mix the clay to some extent. It compresses the clay and eradicates air pockets which are a nuisance in all processes associated with cut or rolled sheets, and which make throwing impossible. The top of a block of clay is rounded by beating with the hands – smacking makes them sore – and the block is then sliced horizontally in two with a wire. The top half is then lifted high, inverted, and the round 'wedge' banged smartly on top of the half remaining on the bench. The illustration clearly demonstrates the compressive force of this action which is repeated – each cut at right angles to the last – a number of times until the cuts themselves reveal that the clay is air-free and homogeneous. There are other methods of both kneading and wedging which differ in detail but not in principle.

With practice a hundredweight or two of clay can be reconditioned by these means in a short space of time, but in a large studio or school, or in a department of a college where much throwing practice is done, there is every justification for some machinery to help with this work (Plate 13). In these circumstances pugmills delivering between three and ten hundredweight of rehashed clay an hour are almost essential, and they also make possible the provision in quantity of interesting mixtures of such clays as Crank Mixture, smooth stoneware clay, red clay and fireclays with or without additional sand or grog.

In spite of the most careful arrangements and supervision of clay storage bone-dry scraps do accumulate. They are best dealt with in small quantities as they occur by breaking down, soaking in excess water over a day or two, and drying on plaster to a kneadable consistency. If the scraps contain other refuse – matches, paper, plaster chips, etc., – the soaked slurry should be sieved before it is dried, and local clays are cleaned of stones and twigs by the same method. The table of clay conditions on page 104 shows that bone-dry clay is the easiest to crush, a leather-hard block being unbelievably strong and resistant to the mightiest blows of pick or hammer.

An awkward factor of reconditioning dry clay, or cleaning local clays, is the space and number of containers required; one bin full of dry clay requires distribution between three or four bins for ease of soaking and stirring, and produces between thirty and forty gallons of slip which has to be dried. Some excess water can be siphoned off after the slip has settled and the drying of the remainder can be hastened to some extent by the addition of new dry powdered clay.

Bibliography to Chapter 4

Chapters in general handbooks:

Bernard Leach, A POTTER'S BOOK.

Vincent Eley, A MONK AT THE POTTER'S WHEEL.

D. M. Billington, THE TECHNIQUE OF POTTERY.

Daniel Rhodes, STONEWARE AND PORCELAIN.

John Newick, CLAY AND TERRACOTTA IN EDUCATION

Discussions in greater detail:–

Daniel Rhodes, CLAY AND GLAZES FOR THE POTTER.

(For further details of all the above books see bibliography to Chapter 6, pages 114 to 117.)

F. H. Norton, ELEMENTS OF CERAMICS. *Addison-Wesley Publishing Co., Inc., Reading, Massachusetts 1952.* A detailed account of the science and technology of clay and other minerals associated with all branches of ceramics. Expensive and intended primarily for the industrial apprentice.

W. E. Worrall, RAW MATERIALS. *Institute of Ceramics Textbook Series, Maclaren & Sons, Ltd. 1964.* Scientific details and much useful geological information.

Chapter 5

Kilns and Firing

Firing is the last process in making a pot or clay model, and it is an exciting conclusion to the work. Few crafts can offer such a satisfactory finale, nor one where the ultimate transformation of the article is so complete, and it is doubtless the fascination of firing which grips the imagination of so many people inside and outside the industry. The glowing vision inside a kiln at its highest temperature is a commanding spectacle, and the test on the material and workmanship of any pot is severe.

If children in schools are to make pots at all then they should be involved in the firing; they should put their own pots into the kiln, help to mind it, and be present at the unloading. They should even build their own kilns. However, like digging all one's own clay, this complete do-it-yourself approach is an ideal which cannot always be carried out. Building and firing a home-made kiln is not difficult and most potters manage to do it sometimes, but to suggest that it is the only way to run pottery classes in schools, or to use pottery as a modelling medium, would be ridiculous. Once children have been started they produce clay models at a surprising rate, and the teacher has every need of an easy and efficient means of completing the products. Electric kilns represent one answer to this problem, and it is possible to arrange that the children take some part in the packing or unloading of the ware, or that they assist in other ways.

It is often suggested for economic reasons that several schools share a kiln, but this is a bad practice which precludes most of the children from becoming deeply involved in the craft. If there can be no alternative to this arrangement it would be advisable not to attempt clay work at all. Kilns certainly are expensive, but no more so than many other items of school equipment, such as projectors, which are considered essential. Perfectly good kilns can be purchased and installed between £80 and £150 depending on the interior size and various extra items of equipment sold with them.

Any fuel can be used to heat a kiln, but electricity has one or two advantages which make it the most suitable for use in schools and very useful in studios. Kilns fired by flame-producing fuels require constant and, especially in the case of gas, skilled attention over a period of ten or twelve hours which many of us find impossible to give. Electric kilns may be left on all night, unattended, and require only to be switched up once or twice during the following day before the final temperature is reached – after several firings the timing can be judged fairly accurately and the time to turn off gauged within an hour or so.

Something is lost in this smooth, almost clinical efficiency, but it is regained in ease and safety and children benefit from fairly rapid completion of their models.

CHOOSING AN ELECTRIC KILN

What are the points to look for in an electric kiln which will be used in a school or a studio?

Size

First of all it is probably the interior size of a kiln which will be considered. Too small a kiln is always a handicap, and a very large one often has to be fired partly empty for the sake of completing work. Sizes such as 15 in. × 12 in. × 12 in., 12 in. × 12 in. × 12 in., 18 in. × 18 in. × 18 in., 21 in. × 21 in. × 15 in., 15 in. × 15 in. × 24 in., are all useful, but if much pottery is being made nothing less than 18 in. × 18 in. × 18 in. will be of any use.

Lids or Doors

Some potters prefer kilns with hinged lids whilst others prefer them with one or two doors at the front. Both types of kiln have advantages and disadvantages. Lidded ones are undoubtedly easy to pack, but the lids are heavy to lift and there is always the danger of one falling if the stay prop is not fixed correctly. Lids also do not often have vents so that steam, and other corrosive gases, can only escape round the edge where they attack the metal hinge and stays, causing rapid wear and tear. Vented lids are supplied if specially requested.

Single doors become rather heavy if the width of the kiln is more than 15 in. so that two doors are preferable on larger models.

Safety Switches

Some kind of safety device on an electric kiln is essential, but padlocks are preferable to door safety switches as the latter sometimes go wrong.

Heat Controls

Another consideration is whether to have a simple 'low-medium-high' switch like an electric cooker hotplate, or to have an 'energy input regulator' which is similar in operation

6

to a simmerstat. Energy regulators are recommended because their lowest setting is lower than the 'low' of the other type of heat control. Low heat is particularly useful with mixed kinds of pottery some of which may be very uneven in thickness, or even slightly damp, at the commencement of a firing. Energy input regulators are, however, an additional expense and are not always reliable.

The two types of heat control operate differently. On the 'low-medium-high' variety at 'low' one-third of the elements are fully alight all the time; at 'medium' two-thirds of them are alight, and all the elements are on at 'full'. Energy regulators are marked in percentages so that at 5 % *all* the elements are fully alight but *only for 5 % of the time*. The elements click on and off continually. This intermittent action makes a low, evenly spread heat possible.

Neither of these types of heat control act as thermostats, but their lowest readings have an apparently similar effect because the heat put into the kiln is ultimately little more than the heat loss. On 'low', or about 30 %, few kilns will reach a temperature above 500° C. even after a day or two. At 'medium', or 60 %, kilns do not seem to reach much above 1000° C., but at 'high', or above 60 %, the maximum rated temperature of the kiln will easily be exceeded and some or all of the elements burned out. These temperatures can only be taken as guides, but they can be safely checked by leaving the kiln at different settings during a day. Low settings will always be safe overnight.

Kilns are not usually fitted with thermostats capable of shutting them off at a given temperature, but a device of this kind has recently been marketed. All potters forget kilns sometimes, but the results are rarely as bad as expected. The two worst accidents known to the author occurred when the responsibility for the firings was passed from one person to another when the final temperatures were almost reached. The author has also heard of a kiln being left at 'medium' for two whole days and nights which was unharmed and had not exceeded high earthenware temperatures. Simpler and cheaper than a thermostat is a red warning light in a place where it is clearly visible.

Maximum Temperatures

Most kilns in schools are not capable of being fired at temperatures higher than 1150° C. or 1250° C. which is a pity considering the small extra cost of one able to reach 1350° C. It is only at temperatures around 1300° C. that natural materials such as ashes, granite or slate, etc., can be used in glazes and young potters should learn to use the materials of their own environment as frequently as possible. High temperatures also bring interesting qualities out of clays and glazes which are obtainable in no other way and which may enhance even the most mediocre objects. Even if most of the firings are to be at low temperatures the elements of a kiln capable of being fired between 1300° C. and 1350° C. will last longer.

Temperature Recording

There are two common methods of recording the temperature inside a kiln; by pyrometer or cones.

Cones – invented by a man called Seger by whose name they are often known – are mixtures of clays and glasses moulded into $2\frac{1}{2}$ in. high cones which are known to *commence* to melt at given temperatures. The cones are set in a stand or pad of clay opposite the spyhole of the kiln, and they can be seen to fall, or bend, when the stipulated temperature is reached. They are reliable and fairly cheap, but they limit the flexibility of shelf arrangements inside the kiln and have to be carefully watched. At high temperatures cones can be difficult to see without a darkened glass.

Pyrometers are more convenient as the temperature rise and fall can be watched throughout the firing and cooling. These instruments work on the principle that a small electric current is induced by heat in a coupled pair of fine wires of certain rare metals. This current is sufficient to induce a magnet to draw a needle across a scale correlated in degrees centigrade. Pyrometers are delicate instruments – especially the thermocouples projecting inside the kiln – and the cheaper models are not always reliable. Before relying on a pyrometer it should be checked several times against cones of different temperatures. Pyrometers cost between £10 and £20.

The better firms offer a variety of sizes of kilns and provide door switches, high temperature elements, energy input regulators and pyrometers as optional extras. Most firms also offer, as an extra, a set of shelves and props, or 'furniture', which it is convenient to buy with the kiln. Replacements of furniture and additional pieces can be bought from a firm of specialists such as Acme Marls Ltd. High temperature furniture is recommended because, though it is more expensive, it does not break so easily.

KILN BUILDING

Building a kiln and firing it is the only way to complete the process of 'teaching with clay', and, being work of a rough physical nature, it is a splendid contrast to the normal routine of school or business life. The work employs many talents and plenty of ingenuity. It is economical, the cost ranging from virtually nothing to about the price of a moderate-sized electric kiln for those made from specially purchased bricks, refractories and firebars. In the following pages details are given of a progression of coal- and wood-fired kilns which are easily built and create considerable interest.

The Biscuit kiln represents the simplest type of up-draught kiln fired essentially with dry twigs. It takes about half-an-hour to build. There is no need to joint the bricks with any form of cement, and the chamber is roofed over – after the pots have been put into position – by corbelling, or overhanging, two or three courses of bricks until a central

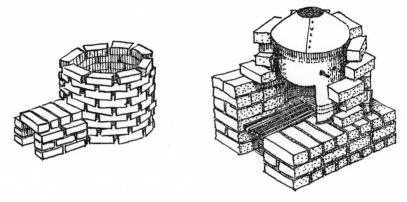

Simple biscuit and raku kilns

hole remains which is small enough to fit a length of old pipe acting as a chimney. Such a kiln will adequately biscuit-fire a few pots or models of coarse clay, but it will not yield a temperature much above 800° C. or tackle glazed wares.

The Raku kiln has some refinements which make possible a higher temperature, but it takes more bricks and a few other parts. It is built on a platform of two or three courses of bricks and the fire is laid on mild steel bars so that the ashes can be cleared whilst it is burning. By resting a metal sheet against the front, above the level of these firebars, the air supply can be directed through the fire from underneath, and it will be pre-heated by the ashes. The kiln is lined with an old five-gallon drum (from which the bottom and half of one side have been removed) to avoid any heat loss through cracks which inevitably occur in bricks arranged in a tight circle, and the chamber is further insulated by using two layers of bricks separated by an earth-filled gap.

If a light conical metal lid is provided this kiln works well for 'Raku' firings which form probably the most dramatic initiation into the mysteries of pottery. In *A Potter's Book* Bernard Leach describes how he first became interested in the art when he took part in a firing of this kind in Japan in 1911. Raku ware is different from all other kinds in that the pots, after they have been biscuited, glazed and decorated, are plunged directly into a red hot kiln and withdrawn as soon as the glaze has formed. They may then be immersed in cold water so that they are ready for instant use.

To do this it is essential to have a long pair of tongs and asbestos gloves, and there are no dangers if the procedure is orderly.*

From cold, and using good dry resinous sticks, the kiln takes about two hours to heat through; the flames are allowed to die down, the chimney and conical lid are removed and the first glazed pots (see page 125 for suitable glaze recipes) placed into a clay container, or

---

* The process could however be VERY DANGEROUS IN ELECTRIC KILNS because heated air is conductive. Forgetting to switch off the current first could be fatal.

'saggar' resting on metal bars or other supports within the kiln. The saggar is needed to protect the ware from the effect of the flames. When the lid and chimney have been replaced the fire is stoked again and kept going hard for about half an hour, after which time it should be evident that the glaze is forming. A hole in the metal cone enables the condition of the glaze to be seen, or the chimney may be removed for a moment with the asbestos gloves. The glaze is deceptive, it will look smooth and glossy whilst it is still bubbling, but experience will tell when it is properly formed.

The raku saggar – or indeed any other kiln parts – need to be made from refractory clay bodies to which a high proportion of grog has been added because of the suddenness of the heating, and, to some extent, this rule applies to all pots or models put into these primitive furnaces where control of the build up of heat is just about impossible. Suitable mixtures for working in were given in a table on page 75 and Crank Mixture would be satisfactory for the saggar. It is possible to use large round tins as saggars, but they do not retain the heat and bend when the fire becomes especially fierce.

The third design is for a coal-fired kiln capable of firing earthenware glaze at 1100° C., and it would provide a potter wishing to make small decorative goods with a workable proposition. The kiln is made from about 300 good quality common bricks without any jointing material, and the design does not require the construction of arches or cutting bricks, though a few half-bricks would help the walling to cross-bond in one or two places. The firebars are lengths of mild steel bar not less than half-an-inch square, and a chimney is provided from a six-foot length of five-inch diameter iron or asbestos pipe, steadied by guy wires. Some means of keeping the firebars separate is also required, and the easiest way would probably be to put projecting bolts at intervals through the two supporting cross bars which are cut from angle metal so that the vertical flange rests in the joint between two side bricks. All the bricks need to be carefully placed and the gaps packed solid with earth or ashes bound with clay. It is essential to start on a levelled patch or slab of concrete.

Whilst building – a job which will take three to four hours – it is advisable to place a ten-inch square kiln shelf in the position shown in the sixth layer so that the flame passage-ways are accurately situated around it in subsequent layers. As earthenware glazes need protection from flames (lead glazes bubble if they are not) firebrick splits are placed around the edge of this shelf, and other shelves, similarly surrounded, are placed on top making a series of saggars to fill the chamber. Firebrick splits $4\frac{1}{2}$ in. high can be bought at most ironmongers, but a variety of distances between the shelves could be obtained if one made one's own saggars from Crank Mixture. Ten-inch earthenware seed pans may also be used.

One of the advantages of this design is that the chimney is not placed centrally and removed for packing, but it is placed at the back of the kiln over a solid pile of brickwork. This has been done by directing the flames from the top of the chamber along a horizontal flue which has the added advantage of slowing their pace so that more heat is retained in the chamber itself. A damper can be made by sliding a sheet of metal, or old kiln shelf, across this flue at the position marked on the plans. Packing can be done by removing the

Up-draught Earthenware Kiln

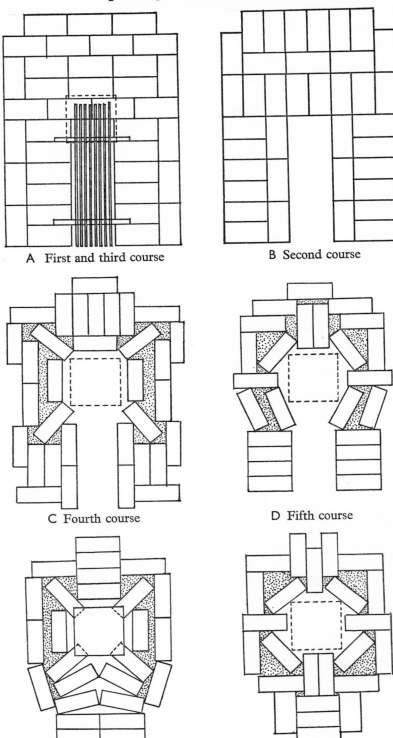

A First and third course

B Second course

C Fourth course

D Fifth course

E Sixth course

F Seventh course

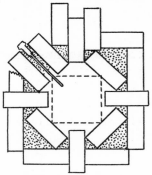

G Eighth and tenth courses

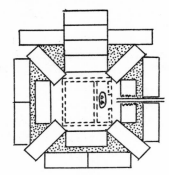

H Ninth course

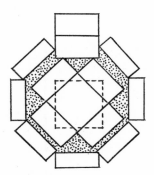

I Eleventh course

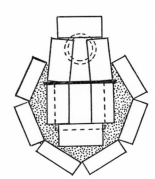

J Twelfth course

A First and third courses showing the firebars and the relative position of ten-inch shelves in the pot chamber above (dotted square). B Second course. Some half-bricks would help to make a better bonding arrangement. C Fourth course showing the foundations of the chamber. The bricks are now stood on edge and the gaps are packed with earth, clay and ashes. D Fifth course completing the firebox height. E Sixth course roofing over the firebox and providing supports for the first kiln shelf or saggar. F Seventh course. G Eight and tenth courses showing possible position for a pyrometer. H Ninth course showing an arrangement for spyhole (iron pipe) and cones. I Eleventh course closing over the chamber. Twelfth course showing the position of the horizontal flue, damper (half-way along). The flue is covered by bricks and earth. The situation of the chimney is also indicated; care should be taken to ensure that its area is not reduced by the brick supports – a six-inch pipe would allow for this bricks which create the flue, and when it is complete the top is insulated with the earth and clay, or ashes and clay mixture.

Temperature recording may be done with cones protected from the flames (cones below 1100° C. suffer in the same way as lead glazes if they are licked by the flames) by being set well back on a shelf as shown in layer 9, but it will be found that a pyrometer teaches one how to stoke because the heat rise and fall can be watched all the time. The temperature rises between stokings, but drops each time new fuel is added until the initial outburst of black smoke has died down. After a period of slowly warming the kiln and the pots – when the damper will be partly closed – the stoking has to be done by small handfuls of coal every other minute until a considerable fire has been built up. Too much new coal at once causes thick black smoke to roll out of the chimney which will justifiably draw complaints from the neighbourhood. The thermocouple of the pyrometer needs protection from the flames, which can be arranged by sliding one or two castellated shelf supports along the exposed part.

The height of this kiln can be increased by repeating one or more of the brick courses, and other similar arrangements of bricks could easily be planned to give greater width to the chamber. However, if anything larger is contemplated an increased fire box will be required, and, as this would need properly shaped pig-iron firebars, it would probably be advisable to build a more permanent kiln capable of a greater variety of work, such as the down-draught one for which sections and isometric drawings are included. This kiln fires easily to high temperature (1300° C.) and is capable of reduction and salt-glaze. It is still easy to build though it will take considerably longer and cost towards £70 if new materials are used throughout.

The down-draught kiln is built with common and firebricks set in fireclay (ordinary cements or mortars are not used in kiln construction), and should be erected on a good foundation of two or three courses of solid brick, or 4 to 6 inches of waterproofed concrete covered around the firemouth area with a layer of firebrick. The fireclay can be used either in the form of a creamy slip into which damped bricks are dipped, or it can be used stiffer, in the more conventional manner known as 'buttering', again on damped bricks. Where creamy slip is used some stiffer clay and sand mixture will be needed for pointing and filling small gaps as the work progresses.

Roofing over and brick arch construction are not always easy problems for the amateur builder, and in any case necessitate the outside of the kiln being bound with wire, or angle-sectioned mild steel, to counter the various thrusts developed. Refractory cement castings have deadweight but no thrust, and therefore simplify building, though a professional builder would look askance at the additional cost and their lack of ability to move with the expanding and contracting brickwork (Plate 14). Refractory cements may be purchased with the correct grade of aggregate already included from several firms around Britain (see list of suppliers), or Ciment Fondu may be used with three parts of a refractory aggregate obtained from a supplier in the reader's district (list available from the manufacturers of Ciment Fondu – see list of addresses). With Ciment Fondu care has to be taken

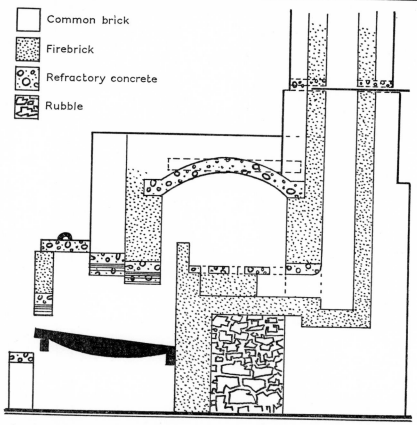

Common brick

Firebrick

Refractory concrete

Rubble

Section of a down-draught high temperature kiln. Scale ½ inch to 1 foot

to soak the aggregate before use, and to see that the mixture is not contaminated with Portland cement. Ciment Fondu with refractory or insulating aggregate would be the ideal material for a base platform cast about 6 inches in thickness. The casting boxes are easily made from scrap timber, and arched shapes can be formed from bent strips of hardboard or plywood. Where other kilns are already available it would not be difficult to make one's own voussoir bricks by ramming a mixture of about half and half fireclay and fireclay grog into wooden moulds and firing before use.

In all the drawings the practice has been adopted of using 9-inch firebrick walls protected by 9 inches of common brick, providing an economical and substantial structure. However, the economy is balanced in terms of brickwork and not heat, which may prove to be false economy in the long run. Where frequent firings are contemplated it would be wise to purchase some more expensive refractory insulation bricks and to build with only 13½ inch walls made from one layer of firebrick, one of insulation and an outer protection of commons. Such refractory insulation bricks as the 'Selfrac' listed among the kiln building

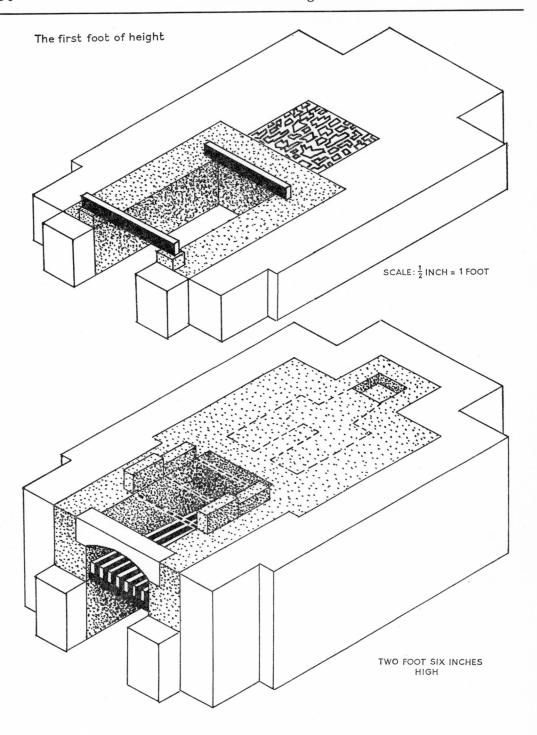

The first foot of height

SCALE: $\frac{1}{2}$ INCH = 1 FOOT

TWO FOOT SIX INCHES HIGH

The next six inches

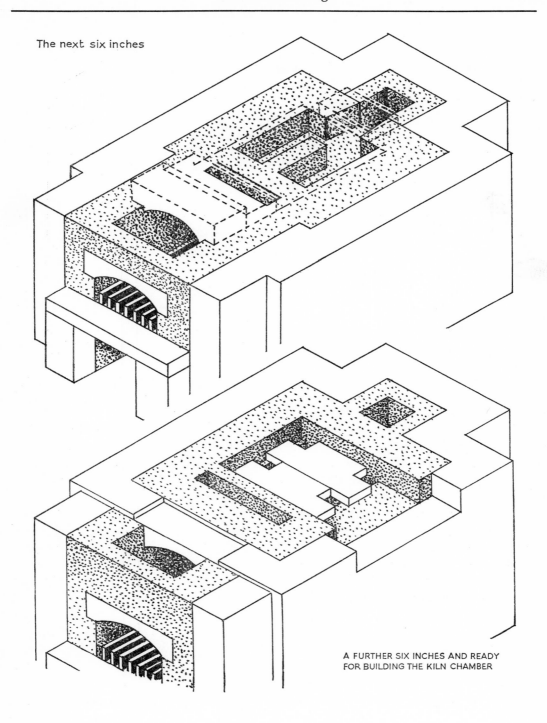

A FURTHER SIX INCHES AND READY
FOR BUILDING THE KILN CHAMBER

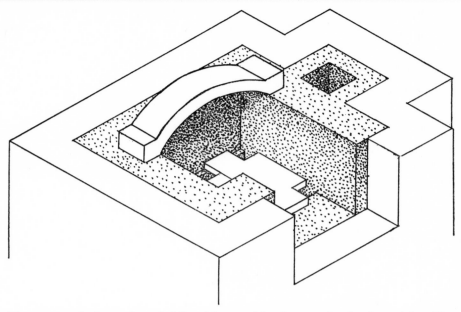

Upper part of a down-draught kiln with one of the three roof arches in position. The walls need to be built level with the top of the arches before the lintels over the door are set in position

materials (page 133) are soft, highly porous, and cost approximately six times as much as common bricks. Where there will be no abrasive action from fire-irons or fuel, such as in the kiln chamber itself, the heat-absorbing firebricks may be dispensed with altogether, and the construction done entirely with Selfrac or similar insulation bricks and commons, with perhaps a gap, filled with ashes bonded with a little clay, between them. Firebricks cost about three times as much as commons and are essential around the fireboxes, though common bricks would do throughout for primitive up-draught or raku kilns where temperatures are never likely to rise beyond that of a good bonfire.

Where alterations of wall structure are contemplated the measurements of the kilns will need changing, and, although the overall measurements are not important, there are some dimensions which cannot be changed without affecting firing performances. In *A Potter's Book* by Bernard Leach there is an interesting discussion on kiln measurements which shows divergences of approach between European and Oriental designers, and other technical papers have been written on the subject which contain important information for the specialist, but which bear only slight relevance to elementary kilns of this type. In general it is important that the flame inlet to the chamber is greater than the outlet to the chimney, and that the cross-sectional area of the chimney should be somewhere between the two. Such an arrangement ensures that the flames and hot gases are not drawn through the kiln with a rush, but are allowed adequate entry and are retained momentarily, to allow complete combustion among the pots, before they are drawn out through the chimney.

Shapes required for building down-draught kiln :-

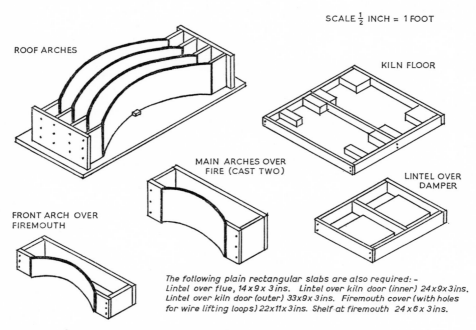

SCALE ½ INCH = 1 FOOT

ROOF ARCHES

KILN FLOOR

MAIN ARCHES OVER
FIRE (CAST TWO)

LINTEL OVER
DAMPER

FRONT ARCH OVER
FIREMOUTH

*The following plain rectangular slabs are also required: -
Lintel over flue, 14 x 9 x 3 ins. Lintel over kiln door (inner) 24 x 9 x 3 ins.
Lintel over kiln door (outer) 33 x 9 x 3 ins. Firemouth cover (with holes
for wire lifting loops) 22 x 11 x 3 ins. Shelf at firemouth 24 x 6 x 3 ins.*

Timber and hardboard moulds for refractory concrete castings

The inlet from the fire to the chamber in this down-draught kiln is 24 inches by 4 inches, the six slots in the floor have a total area of 60 square inches (in the floor itself these measure 100 square inches, but they are reduced by the projecting brickwork supporting the floor underneath), the underfloor flue to the chimney is 6 inches by 9 inches, and the chimney has a cross-sectional area of 9 inches by 9 inches. This gives the following ratio of areas through which the flames pass:

Main inlet	*Outlet through floor*	*Inlet to chimney*	*Chimney*
96	60	54	81

The outlets through the floor can be reduced in area, if this is felt necessary, and the total volume of the pot chamber can be increased by two or three additional courses of bricks without materially impairing the performance of the kiln.

The height of the chimney is important, but it depends to some extent on the air circulation of the site and, in built-up areas, on council by-laws. The height can easily be altered by the addition or subtraction of courses of brickwork which could even be carried out during a firing. Ten feet from the ground should be adequate in most situations. Tapering flues are said to be superior to straight-sided ones.

The control of draught and air supply needs careful consideration. In this design provision has been made for a shelf level with the firebars so that the air entering above the fire can be controlled separately from the air entering between the bars from underneath. Air rushing across the top of the fire will only cool the kiln so that this gap is progressively *closed* during firing with several bricks, being opened only for cleaning the fire. A removable cover must be provided on top for refuelling, and it is suggested that strong iron loops are provided in holes cast with the slab through which an iron lifting bar can be slid. The iron loops cannot be cast in place because their expansion would crack the slab. Air passing through the fire from under the bars aids combustion and is, in any case, pre-heated as it passes over the hot ashes. The lower entrance is also closed with bricks and will be progressively *opened* during the firing. When the firing is finished cold air is allowed to pass over the remains of the fire until it has burned out.

Dampers are essential for controlling the early rush of temperature rise, and for stopping sudden cooling at the end. Provision is made in the chimney above the kiln roof by setting two lintels having a channel underneath through which a metal plate can slide. Dampers are also essential during reduction firing when excess gases are needed within the chamber to attack the hot clays and glazes.

The kiln chamber doors are similarly closed with bricks, and it is advisable to lay these, without any jointing material, whilst building the chamber so that a doorway is created suitable for filling with standard-sized bricks. Doors are not jointed with fireclay during firings though the outside surfaces are generally smeared all over (clamming) to prevent cold air entering through small cracks, the presence of which can be located by closing the damper for a few moments when the fire has just been stoked. An observation hole must be left in the door to ensure the visibility of cones and another hole will be needed for a pyrometer thermocouple.

Firebars may be of mild steel only in low temperature kilns; any better or more permanent construction requires cast pig-iron bars, properly shaped and resting on two substantial crossbars. Most districts have an iron foundry whose workmen are familiar with this problem, and second-hand sets can often be purchased – the railways will be discarding them for some time yet. New firebars can be expensive and estimates should be sought before an order is placed. Two long-handled fireirons will also be required, a poker for clearing the gaps between the bars and a rake for occasionally pulling the ashes to the front of the firemouth.

Any kiln to be used continuously requires some protection from rain and snow, though they would be unpleasant to fire if they were completely enclosed. A lean-to of the kind showing in Plate 15 is perfectly adequate, and the outside common brickwork of the kiln can be pointed with a cement and sand mix to give added protection for the clay joints. Chimneys should be covered between firings to prevent moisture penetrating into the absorbent interior brickwork. Bricks which have been given elementary protection in this way may be used time and time again on different kilns.

It will be difficult to resist lighting a fire before the last bricks have been placed, but it is wise to clean the site around the kiln beforehand, and to arrange that the fuel is conveniently situated – and under cover – before the excitement commences. The first firing must be very slow in order to dry the kiln structure thoroughly, and it is best to proceed by lighting a small fire for an increasing length of time over several days before the real firing is commenced.

PACKING

Kiln packing can be a lengthy and tricky job, but it is made easier, and may be done without much wasted space, if several sizes of shelf are available. Some shelves the full area of the kiln are useful, but others of half and quarter this area allow tall pots to be placed in corners with the smaller ones between shelves. The 9 or 10 inch square shelves and 9 by 6 inch plain tile CRANKS are exceptionally useful with the variety of children's work, and space can be saved between them by using DOTS as supports instead of CASTELLATED PROPS. For general use, however, the two sizes of castellated prop cannot be improved upon. Broken shelves should never be discarded as they seem often to fit where a whole one will not.

Pots are usually fired twice. The first time, known as the BISQUE or BISCUIT fire, rids the clay of water and other gaseous matter, leaving it in a strong and porous state which can

Above: biscuit packing with shelves and a 'bung' of similar sized ware. *Below:* the same pots disposed for a glaze firing using stilts where necessary

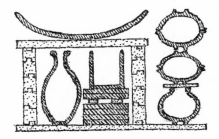

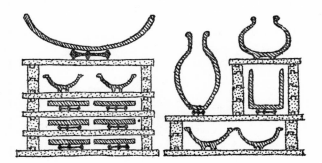

easily be glazed. A satisfactory temperature for this firing would be 1050° C. After the ware has been dipped in glaze suspension it is fired again at a suitable temperature for the glaze.

During the biscuit fire the pots may touch one another and be piled up in BUNGS. It should be remembered, however, that clay expands before it shrinks in firing, and care has to be taken to ensure that pots do not settle into one another so that they become locked together as they contract. Oxides painted on the surfaces tend to spread to adjacent pots so those decorated in this way need to be kept separate.

During the glaze fire the pots should not touch one another, nor should the glazed surfaces touch the kiln walls or furniture. Three-pointed STILTS of various sizes are sold to stand the pots away from the shelves, and a selection of sizes is necessary. Some models cannot stand on stilts so that they must be sponged clear of glaze underneath and a little way up the sides in case the glaze runs down. Broken pieces of shelf may again be useful for awkward models.

Careless glaze packing can lead to costly damage of the shelves as well as the pots. It is advisable to paint shelves with a good coating of an infusible wash consisting of equal parts of china clay and flint, mixed in water, and sieved into a smooth cream like distemper. This wash prevents glaze droplets from sticking very hard and should always be used at high temperatures to prevent the clay bases from fusing to the shelves. When accidents do occur the glaze – or pot – should be chipped off lightly with a hammer and chisel, and the damaged shelf ground with a carborundum stone before rewashing. Chipping off is a dangerous operation for which it is essential to wear glasses and to be away from other people. Droplets of glaze and broken tips of stilts embedded in the bases of pots are also liable to cut fingers, and carborundum stones are again used for grinding them smooth. Stilts cannot be used for more than one or two firings.

If the firing is to be above 1200° C. the packing should be done with care. Towards 1300° C. most clays become soft and partly molten, so that adequate support for the shelves is very necessary; a shelf 17 in. by 17 in. by $\frac{1}{2}$ in. may well be supported in three places during an earthenware firing, but at high temperatures five supports are needed for a shelf of this size. At high temperatures three supports would be adequate for 10 in. squares ($\frac{1}{2}$ in. thick), but the thin ($\frac{1}{4}$ in.) tile cranks again need five points of support in the form of dots. Even with adequate support shelves may warp so that they rock in future packings, but rocking can be overcome by using some of the rising supports sold with castellated props. Stilts are not generally used in high temperature firings as the weight of the pots tends to bed the points very firmly into the bases and they may even poke right through thin pots.

FIRING

The most important point to remember in firing is that it should be done slowly. An average heat rise of 150° C. per hour would be considered very fast, and even at this rate only 1050° C. could be achieved during the normal school day of 9 a.m. to 4 p.m. It is essential, therefore, to fire slowly overnight so that the kiln is between 400° C. and 550° C. by 9 a.m.

Several changes of crystal structure and chemical composition take place during the heating of clay, and if the speed of heating is too great cracks will occur due to the stress of these changes, or the clay may disintegrate with an audible explosion. These accidents are most likely to occur when chemically combined water is being driven from the molecules of clay between 300° C. and 550° C. When this 'water of formation' has gone the clay can no longer return to mud when it is wetted. Reversions of crystal structure also take place during cooling, so that the speed of this stage should not be forced either. An important change takes place at 230° C. and patience is needed whilst the temperature falls below this point.

Firing speeds and temperatures are discussed in detail at technical meetings in industry or in text books for manufacturers, but it must be remembered that their problems are very different from those faced by a teacher in a school. Dinner plates or lidded tureens etc. in china, or even white earthenware, present difficulties of distortion or warping which are hardly likely to be detected if they occur in a child's model or an individual studio piece. The firing of large kilns filled with delicately made wares is indeed a highly skilled and specialized trade to which the firing of a small electric kiln bears no resemblance.

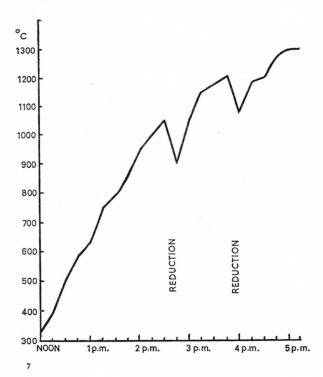

Graph of a successfully reduced stoneware firing in the downdraught high temperature kiln illustrated. The temperatures were recorded on a pyrometer every 15 minutes (later every 7½ mins.), and it is difficult to learn the art of stoking without such help. Loss of temperature when the damper is closed for reduction is to be expected.

7

Firings must inevitably fit in with the school routine, and wares will come to no harm if the few simple rules outlined above are observed.

A note should be added on solid fuels as most home-made kilns will be fired with them. These fuels supply heat from the conversion of carbon into carbon monoxide or dioxide, and one would expect the greatest efficiency from the fuel containing the highest proportion of this element. However, the reverse is true because the efficiency of a fuel depends on oxygen supplies and few home-made kilns have sufficient draught to derive much benefit from the high concentration of carbon in coke. Experimental home-made kilns are inevitably inefficient furnaces making use of little more than one-tenth of the possible heat output of the fuel, and for this reason the fuel from which the heat energy is most easily released is likely to give the best results. However, seasoned dry timber for burning is not easily provided in large quantities and coal is the next best. Hard small coal will give good results fed a little at a time towards the back of a good glowing fire. The fire needs to be cleaned at intervals with a long-handled rake, and the observations already made (page 94) on the operation of firemouth and ashpit doors should be followed with care. Fitting a drip-feed oil-burner which can be left unattended for long periods should not be a difficult operation. Where wood is to be used it must be graded in size according to the kiln, small ones, such as the Biscuit or Raku kilns described earlier, require twigs no larger than one inch in diameter.

Bibliography to Chapter 5

Chapters in general handbooks including plans and notes on kiln building:–

William Ruscoe, A MANUAL FOR THE POTTER.

Bernard Leach, A POTTER'S BOOK.

Daniel Rhodes, STONEWARE AND PORCELAIN.

Murray Fieldhouse, POTTERY.

(For further details of the books above see bibliography to Chapter 6, pages 114 to 117.)

Paul Soldner, KILN CONSTRUCTION. American Craftsmen's Council 1965 (available from Tiranti – see list of addresses, page 137). A well produced, slender, pamphlet, expensive by British standards, but full of interesting ideas and information. Most of the kilns discussed are gas fired.

Denise and Rosemary Wren are prepared to sell detailed plans and notes of their well-known coke-fired high-temperature kilns which have been in use for many years. The sum of £3 covers the cost of the plans and the right to build one of each design. Write, enclosing cheque, to D. and R. Wren, The Oxshott Pottery, Potters' Croft, Oakshade Road, Oxshott, Surrey.

Chapter 6

Making and Decorating

Children and most adults take to working with clay quite easily and quickly invent their own ways of forming it. However, sound working methods take a long time to develop unaided, and the material has some traits which always cause disappointments to the unwary. Before we go on to discuss the simple methods of working and decorating clay, therefore, it may be as well to call attention to the common snags with four rules which cannot be broken:

1. Soft clay cannot be attached to harder clay, nor can clay of one texture be attached to clay of another because of differences of shrinkage.

2. Any piece of a model much larger than a golf ball must be hollow and, if an air space is enclosed, a hole must be provided to allow for the escape of expanding air and steam caused by heating. Even though a model may appear perfectly dry when it is placed in the kiln, steam is generated by chemical changes within the clay and it cannot escape from the interior of a large solid piece. (See page 35.) Coarse clays like Crank Mixture allow more latitude in this respect because they are porous.

3. Pieces of clay to be joined must be scratched, coated with slip, and carefully welded together. The reason for this is obvious, but children have a tendency to merely 'place' a head on a neck and are often casual about fixing legs or tails. Slip is clay reduced to a liquid consistency and the scratching helps it to soften the surfaces before the pieces are joined. *Only pieces of clay that are fairly damp can be joined successfully.*

4. Finished models or pots should be dried as slowly as possible, away from draughts or currents of warm air. (See also the notes on firing.)

Though clays of unequal shrinkage will part before the model reaches the kiln, the remainder of the workmanship is tested very severely in the firing. In this respect pottery is akin to baking and the results after heating are equally transformed!

Monkey on a donkey. Greek, late 6th
century B.C.

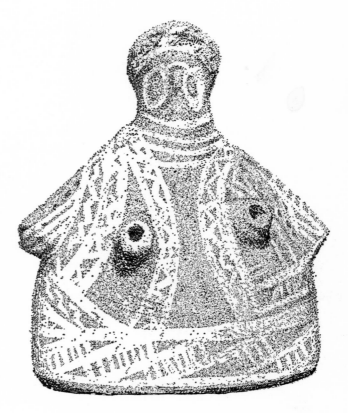

Bust. Early Minoan, 2500–2100 B.C.

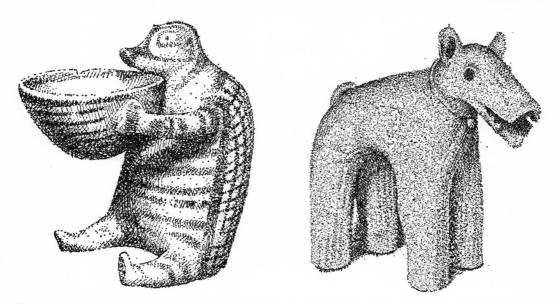

The robust simple forms of good clay models are apparent in these two models and those on the opposite page. *Left:* a bear drinking. From Syros, 2–3000 B.C. *Right:* dog. From Japan, 300–600 A.D.

MAKING

The robust simple forms of good clay models result from working cleanly and directly in a soft plastic material; the more direct and straightforward the technique the more likelihood of success. Directness of technique can only come from working with clay which has some form to start with; the sticky congealed mess of an untidy clay bin, or the twisted scrap torn off a block by hand, have little in common with animate or inanimate forms around us and do singularly little to spark off the imagination. How different is the tidy block! It can be cut swiftly into sheets or cubes, and the sheets cut again smartly into strips or squares. In a second the cubes are beaten into balls and, perhaps, the balls flattened into discs or elongated and rolled into rods.

Each simple solid form has infinite uses; the sheet gives the pieces of an engine (Plate 33), the walls of a castle, the roof of a house, the wings of an aeroplane, a plate, the bottom of a pot or the base of a model. When wrapped round a rolling pin it yields a vase (Plate 17); round a block of wood it yields a box, and when wrapped round the fingers it may be carefully pressed and modelled into the body of an animal. On its own, unbent and uncurled, the sheet is a surface for decorative experiment, a tile, a piece of mosaic or a wall plaque.

The cube and other rectangular shapes offer the same freedom; they can be hollowed with ease to form troughs or carriages, lorries, houses, dolls cupboards and so forth (Plate

19). Solid, and on a slightly larger scale, blocks are the commonest clay forms of all – bricks.

The sphere which one beats out of a cube is the start of the wealth of thrown forms, and it can be useful in hand modelling. Small bowl shapes can be pinched out quickly (Plate 34) and either finished carefully as pots, or they can be made in pairs and attached to one another by the rims to become bodies, piggie-banks, vases or whistles.

The largest pots or figures can be built up layer upon layer by the use of strips or rolls (Plates 20, 21 and 22). An article appeared in *Pottery Quarterly* (No. 14, Summer 1957) describing a Korean potter making ten or twelve immense storage jars a day by this method, and it is a method used by contemporary studio potters for building large or asymmetrical pots which cannot be made on a wheel.

Directness of technique also depends on the condition of the clay and an attempt has been made to describe in words the various conditions suitable for different processes in a table (page 104). The sheet that is too soft cannot be handled in any way and yields nothing, and a hard ball of clay certainly cannot be pinched into a bowl. Clay that is in the right condition does not stick, nor does it crack when you bend it and, when bent, it is firm enough to remain in position without collapsing. At the same time there are occasions when soft or, more frequently, harder pieces are necessary, and a half completed model will often need stiffening before the final touches can be done. Experience can be the only guide.

Similarly, experience helps with the swift making of sheets; they may be rolled out like pastry or they may be cut like cheese. Cutting is obviously the quicker method, but rolling compresses the clay and gives the sheet a little added strength or plasticity. Working from a large block of clay one can compromise by cutting a sheet a little too thick and rolling it down to the desired measurement. Cutting is done with a wire stretched across a U-shape of springy metal; the wire is attached to the metal equidistant from the ends of both prongs, and several cutters should be available with wires at different distances so that various thicknesses of clay may be obtained. When the cutter is held upright the wire is parallel with the bench and may be drawn through a piece of clay; the surplus clay on top is then lifted away and the sheet remains on the bench. If the clay is too soft the surplus will not lift off the sheet, nor will the sheet lift off the bench. Large sheets, perhaps above 10 inches square, are not easy to handle whatever their condition, and the block should be placed on a square of hessian or cloth before it is cut so that the sheet has some support whilst it is moved. Clay does tend to stick to unabsorbent surfaces such as lino, formica, or zinc, and any work of this kind is more easily carried out on smooth concrete (Plate 13), wood or sheets of asbestos.

Cutting a sheet of clay

Formers used for bending sheets into various hollow cross-sections should first be

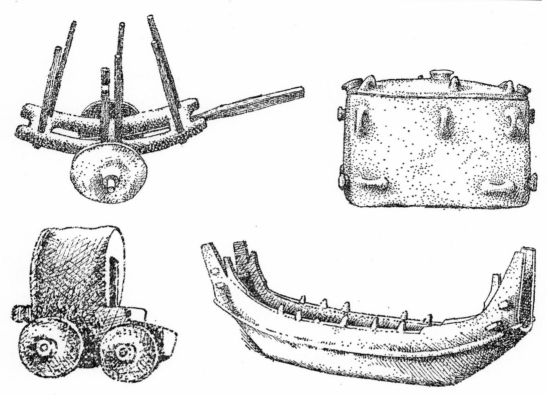

Four drawings depicting a variety of objects constructed from flat pieces of clay. *Top left:* a cart from Mohenjo-Daro 2500–2100 B.C., suggesting the possibilities of combining wood and clay. *Top right:* burial urn from the Minoan civilisation (c. 1800 B.C., length 30 inches) noticeably lacking in the harsh angular quality associated with sheet or slab construction. *Bottom left:* a Scythian cart, about 600 B.C. *Bottom right:* a boat from Japan, 300–600 A.D.

wrapped in newspaper so that they may be easily withdrawn before the clay begins to shrink. The newspaper will probably remain inside the clay, but it may be left to burn away in the biscuit firing. A collection of timber offcuts of different sections and sizes is invaluable for this method.

The best instrument for cutting clay is a needle mounted in a wooden handle. An ordinary knife blade, though it may be sharp, has a thickness of metal behind the cutting edge which tends to drag in the clay; where potters use knives they are lean and pointed. Tiles can only be accurately cut when the clay is a little too stiff to bend, and mosaic pieces are better half cut through, like pieces of chocolate, and snapped apart when they are dry.

Tiles, or other flat pieces of clay, warp as they dry because the edges dry and shrink before the centre. Slow drying with frequent turning on to dry boards is helpful, but again

The Various Conditions of Good Pottery Clay

	Description	Uses
Slurry	Thin, free running, liquid.	Easy to sieve.
Slip		
Thin	Consistency of light cream.	Gives thin coatings by dipping.
Medium	Thick cream, but flows easily round container.	Ideal for coating insides of pressed dishes by pouring in and then emptying.
Thick	Sluggish movement in bowls but moderately easy to stir.	Rather thick for dipping, but excellent for application through slip trailer.
Heavy	Little fluidity and heavy to stir.	Jointing medium or for decoration applied by brush.
Plastic		
Sticky	Sticks to bench and fingers.	—
Soft	Barely inclined to stick to bench etc.	Useful consistency in which to knead two different clays together, or to add grog.
GOOD	EASILY SQUEEZABLE; NOT STICKY; REMAINS IN SHAPE.	PINCHING, COILING, THROWING, WRAP-AROUND POTS, ETC.
Stiff	Firm but still squeezable. Inclined to crack when bent.	Pressed dish-making; embossed decoration.
Leather		
Damp	Quite damp, but cannot be bent or modelled without cracking.	Slab pots, hollowed-out pots or models, carved work. Condition in which handles or other attachments are applied; for making inlaid tiles, carrying out inlaid decoration on pots or dipping pots in slip.
Dry	Distinct shrinkage due to loss of moisture. The strongest pre-fired condition.	The last possible stage during which repairs can be effected. Condition suitable for carrying out sgraffito decoration provided slip or oxide coating was applied earlier.
Hard	Showing lighter colour on edges etc.	—
White Hard	Lightest colour appeared all over but likely to be damp inside.	—
Bone Dry	Brittle and ready for firing. Known as 'green ware'.	Easiest condition in which to break up large lumps preparatory to soaking down again.

coarse porous clay will give the best results. Commercial white tiles are made by compressing dry clay dust into a steel mould under considerable pressure so that the problem of warping does not arise.

Sheets of clay may be cut and joined like wood, but the joints have to be made carefully. Both surfaces to be joined should be scratched and liberally coated with slip of the same clay. After they have been pressed together it is advisable to weld a thin coil of clay into the internal corner and to burnish over the exterior surface of the join with a modelling tool. Jointing together five or six sheets of clay is a tedious method of making a hollow cube; small ones may be shaped solid and dug out with a looped wire modelling tool, and larger ones may first be cut in half to make the interior more accessible, the two halves being rejoined with slip.

On a large scale the idea of forming models solid and hollowing them afterwards has

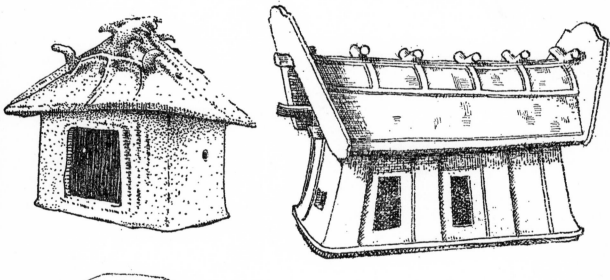

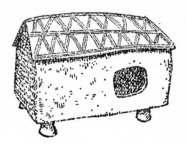

Intriguing models of houses are to be found all over the world. *Top left:* Etruscan, 9th–10th centuries B.C. *Top right:* Japanese, 300–600 A.D. *Bottom left:* Chinese farmhouse, 1st century A.D. *Bottom right:* Central European, Iron Age

great possibilities, but with small, hand-sized models there is a danger that it may lead to the appearance of dull lifeless forms having all the weaknesses of imitation, instead of the simplicity and strength that spring naturally from the re-interpretation of the forms of other materials into those characteristic of clay.

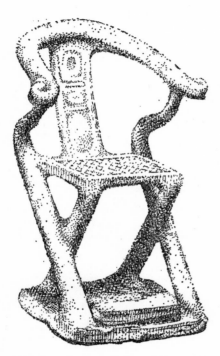

'. . . the reinterpretation of forms of other materials into those characteristics of clay' Chinese, Han dynasty

Pinching is a very natural clay technique, but some practice is required before a good, even, cup or bowl form can be made. Uneven pinching creates a wavy rim; for accuracy the initial ball should be well rounded and the thumb forced gently down the centre. The walls are then thinned by slowly pinching between the thumb and forefinger whilst the bowl is turned in the other hand. If cracks appear on the rim they should be smoothed across with a clean dry finger; moisture is only used if the trouble persists and the clay no longer feels plastic. Oriental potters perfected this simple method centuries ago and used it to produce a surprising range of subtle and well formed drinking bowls. Two pinched bowls of the same diameter can be stuck together with a little slip and the joint welded over to form a hollow sphere. A hole is then cut through which a finger is inserted to weld over the internal joint, and the sphere may then be beaten into a more suitable shape for an animal's body. Additional forms may be added with coils or strips.

The accurate and swift rolling of coils also depends, to some extent, on the shape they are started from. A cylinder is no use because the outer layer of clay expands first leaving the inner core behind forming hollow ends. It is better to take a cube or ball and beat it until it is cigar-shaped, round in section with tapered ends; this should then be rolled gently on the bench to ensure perfection of form before pressure is applied to expand it. Few people in fact roll these cigars, they rock them back and forth and hence need to turn them over frequently to prevent the formation of oval or even square sections. As the coil expands keep the whole length moving by working rhythmically and slide the hands up and down the length to anneal the surface of the clay. Always keep the ends tapered and light otherwise they will flap about and break the rhythmical motion. A practised hand can soon roll a coil 6 feet long and half an inch thick.

Coils can be assembled in many ways; the easiest method is probably to use thick ones beaten into flat strips and welded together, edge to edge. One end of a strip is cut to a shamfer and the other is welded to this face before the surplus is cut off. Coil building is certainly one of the most flexible building techniques, and it can be employed on any shape or scale.

Coil building. Coils are easily rolled in three stages; first the blocks are beaten into fat cigar shapes, they are then rolled out to the required thickness and finally flattened with the edge of the hand. In the drawing the texture caused by the fingers welding the joins is clearly visible on the pot, and the surplus end of the coil is ready to be cut off flush with the surface. Few tools are required for this useful process

One last method of hollow building which is especially suitable for heads or bodies is to build on to a ball of wet newspaper which is not quite as large as the finished article is intended to be. Because of its soft spongy nature the wet newspaper allows the clay to contract and, provided there are adequate vent holes in the model, the paper may be left inside to burn away in the kiln.

Shallow dishes are enjoyable surfaces to decorate, and they are made on one-piece moulds into – or over – which sheets of clay are pressed (Plates 35 and 37). Pottery moulds should be porous so that the clay does not stick to them and they are usually made of plaster. However, to avoid the complications of introducing this material into small workshops or classrooms, moulds can be made from Crank Mixture and fired before use.* In some ways biscuit-fired moulds are superior to plaster, they are stronger, less inclined to chip, and have a character which is more in keeping with clay itself.

None of these techniques requires many tools, though there are three additional items of equipment which help in schools where the working time is strictly limited each week. These items are a greenhouse spray which will provide a misty cloud of vapour for damping models which have become a little too dry; a fan heater or some other device for quickly stiffening models which are a little too damp to work on, and an airtight 'damp-cupboard' for keeping models in the same condition from week to week. Biscuit tins serve well as damp storage when used upside down with the tin acting as a cover over models placed

* Fragments of plaster ruin clay because they blow out in the firing.

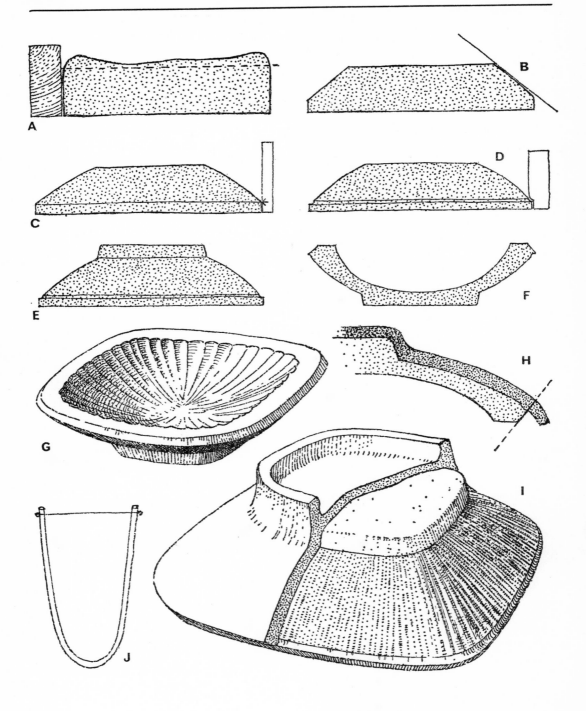

A

B

C

D

E

F

G

H

I

J

KEY TO DIAGRAM

Making the mould for the dish shown in plate 37.

A A block of coarse clay was prepared and beaten into shape with a plank

B After the top had been carefully levelled some surplus was cut off the sides with a wire. The clay was then allowed to stiffen.

C The slope of the sides was made accurate by using a scraper or saw blade, and a horizontal line established with the aid of a marked stick. In this case a texture was applied to the sloping sides at this stage

D A rim moulding being scored with a notched stick

E An additional piece of clay applied with slip to form a central well in the finished dish

F The mould turned over and hollowed with a looped wire tool after which a bevelled edge was shaved accurately down to the moulding. When quite dry the mould was biscuit fired

G The finished mould upside down

H To make a dish, a clay sheet is prepared on damp cloth and pressed firmly over the mould using a smooth wooden block, After the cloth has been removed the surplus clay is trimmed away from the edge with a stretched ox-bow wire (J) resting on the bevel of the mould. The correct angle for this bevel on any mould is such that the wire cuts the clay at approximately a right angle

I The completed dish with added foot ready to be lifted off the mould. Lifting off is easy when the clay has stiffened a little, but in this case if the dish was left too long the clay shrunk firmly on to the mould and cracked. Pressed dishes should be finally dried, rim down, on a flat surface.

Simpler moulds are made by omitting stages D and E and most pressed dishes are satisfactory without added feet on the lid, but a permanent zinc-lined cupboard with flexible shelf arrangements will always be useful. A large school may well need a small room lined with shelves and with a concrete floor which can be soaked.

The first item of equipment installed in so many schools is a throwing wheel. Unless the teacher is himself an expert thrower, the mere presence of a wheel seems to act as a brake on the imaginative use of other techniques of pot-making. The potters' wheel is hypnotic; on the films or television it appears easy to use, but throwing is, in fact, a difficult job. It demands more skill than probably any other craft process and rewards only those who can practise for hours and days on end. The wheel also demands a physique that young children do not have.

DECORATING

Decoration must be considered during the making, but so often students are diffident about it because they say they have no ideas, or are afraid of spoiling what they have already achieved. These unfortunate feelings generally arise from misconceptions about the meaning of 'decoration' which conjures images of branches of ivy leaves or bouquets of flowers such as we often see on commercial wares. Decoration is applied to a pot to enhance its surface and to define its form. There are many ways of approaching the task and very few rules; the best schemes are often unbelievably simple, and may involve nothing more than a slight change of texture over one area, or a single band of colour round a rim. With inhibited students it is probably wise to discard the word decoration, and to talk of 'surface treatment' which describes more precisely what is meant.

Clay surfaces can be textured, patterned or coloured in many ways, and effects may be achieved ranging from naturalistic imitation in full colour, such as we have already mentioned, to the roughest textures reminiscent of boiling lava. The methods of applying decoration fall conveniently into three categories corresponding to the different stages of firing a pot: there are a number which are completed before the pot is fired at all, some are executed between biscuit and glaze firing, and others again are carried out on the fired glaze and sealed to it by an additional firing at a low temperature. Industrial tableware is generally decorated by this latter process, known as 'enamelling' or 'on-glaze', because it is admirably suited to printing or other mass production techniques on smooth white clay wares. At the low temperature of the enamel fire (750° C. to 800° C.) it is possible to obtain a wide range of colours, including gold or other lustres, and the best of this type of ware is very pleasing.

However, the hesitant student will feel happier decorating during the excitement of making the pot, and will gain confidence from working directly on the clay before it is fired. Soft clay asks to be indented and one's instinctive reaction to a block is to poke it with a finger. Here surely is a fundamental approach to surface treatment from which a wealth of textures or patterns may grow unconsciously, and apparently without effort. One

Spontaneous finger decorations by a Roman workman, 2nd century A.D.

realizes immediately that other instruments are even more effective prodders than the fingers, and what starts as a trickle of ideas evolved from the hand turns inevitably into a torrent as handbags or pockets are turned out for the sake of the varied patterns to be derived from their contents. Every potter should collect his own tools; the search becomes fascinating and many an old gear cog, hexagonal bolt or discarded electrical fitting will be rescued from the scrap heap (Plate 20). More personal impressing tools may be made from wood, or from clay, in which case they will be fired before use (Plate 16).

There is, unfortunately, a limit to the usefulness of this discovery because so many pots will be too dry and hard to be indented by the time the making is completed. These pots can still, however, be scratched or engraved, and one finds again that discarded tools, or other oddments from such places as the kitchen drawer, can have another spell of useful life. Old saw blades are of great value and stonemasons' claws, pastry cutters, butter patters, leather tools or umbrella frames have also been regularly employed in this way, but it will be found that pointed tools like clay cutting needles make unpleasant incisions with sharp burr on the edges. The successful engraving tools are those which cut a V or U channel, showing light on one side and shadow on the other (Plate 36).

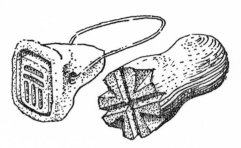

Clay and wooden impressing tools

Scratched or indented decorations may look and feel unpleasant over forms which are broken by minor undulations caused by fingers during the making. Such lumps and hollows may be levelled by scraping in different directions when the clay is leather-hard with a steel 'palette' or 'kidney', though sometimes it may be easier to use a toothed tool, such as a broken hacksaw blade, and to remove the toothmarks when the surface is true by the use of a palette. Scraping with a saw blade, especially if it has been done rhythmically, may be decoration enough for the form, and there are occasions where the finger marks caused in building – most likely during coiling or strip-building – are sufficiently even and rhythmical to merit leaving alone.

Such simple techniques depend for their effect on the play of light, and they may be spoiled by the wrong glaze. Scratched decoration can feel pleasant when burnished with a modelling tool and unglazed, but otherwise such pots should receive a coloured transparent glaze which collects in the lines and shows dark, or an opaque one which, when high-fired, draws away from the edges of the decoration revealing a brown line. (See frontispiece.)

A demand will soon be made for colour which may be provided in three ways. Different colours of liquid clays (slips) provide an earthy range which is particularly pleasant under the traditional iron-stained, honey-coloured, transparent glaze (see frontispiece). White slip can be stained to almost any colour by the addition of various metal oxides, but the method is not appealing; blues and greens, etc., are best obtained by the use of oxides direct on the clay under a white opaque glaze (see frontispiece), or left to be provided by the third source of colour which is the glaze itself.

There are no difficulties in preparing either slips or oxides. Dry clay powder needs only to be crushed, soaked, and brushed through an 80 mesh sieve to provide a slip, and a black one may be made by adding 6 or 8 % of iron oxide and about 4 % of manganese oxide to some red clay powder before it is soaked. Black is the only colour that goes well with the red, buff or white of the other natural clays. Pots may be dipped into slip, or it may be painted on, or trailed through some apparatus similar to a surgical injector or an icing bag.

Oxide powders are mixed with water and ground with a palette knife on a tile, but there is less waste if a tablespoonful or two is ground with water in a pestle and mortar and stored in a labelled and lidded jar. Labelling of jars is vital because all the colouring oxides except iron – cobalt for blues, copper for green and manganese for purple – are black powders. They may be mixed together in varying proportions to provide a greater range of colour, and they mostly need to be applied rather thinly – like ink – because they work by forming a crystal structure within the white glaze. If too much is used the result fires to a blackened and blistered mess, and one has more control over thickness of application if the brush is worked out on a tile beforehand. Oxides are usually applied to the glaze after it has been coated on the biscuit and before it is fired, but this technique is difficult and they work perfectly satisfactorily underneath the glaze.

Scratched decoration may be inlaid with slips or oxides (Plates 28, 29 and 35), and impressed patterns look particularly well when filled with slip and coated with coloured transparent glaze. In order to fill the decoration the slips or oxides are brushed liberally over the whole pot and, when dry, the surface is scraped clean with a steel palette. Several coats of slip may be needed before the pattern is filled, but one coat of any oxide should suffice. The operation can only be done cleanly if the pot is leather-hard; if it is too dry the sudden wetting of the surface may cause cracks which cannot be remedied.

The choice of glaze is all-important. At stoneware temperature many exquisite surfaces can be obtained which require no embellishment (see frontispiece), but at the lower temperatures of earthenware the glazes do not contribute so much to the ware. Indications have already been given about the appropriate use of coloured transparent glazes and white opaques, and for general ease of running, where storage space is short, it is better to rely on these glazes alone, obtaining variety of effect from the clay, slips, oxides or temperature variations.

All the decorative techniques discussed are completed before biscuit-firing and this simplifies the organization of pottery classes considerably. With earthenware it is perfectly obvious after biscuiting which glaze a pot or model requires, and it can be applied by the teacher without any further reference to the maker. It is, of course, preferable for students to do their own glazing, as it is indeed with any other side of the work, but in a school it is not always possible for the student to be present at the crucial moment when some spaces have to be filled in a kiln.

Many models look better unglazed and fired at a temperature high enough to bring out the best colour in the clay (see frontispiece). Glazes, especially opaque ones, tend to fill in fine detail and cause highlights all over the form which can upset its simplicity.

The distribution of decoration over the form requires conscious thought, though one can lay down no hard and fast rules. In general a pattern should not run from one clearly defined area of the surface to another, and a suitable position can sometimes be decided by seeing which part of the surface is visible when the pot is viewed from a normal position, such as table height, whilst one is standing. Shallow bowls, whose interiors alone are visible, should obviously be decorated there and round-bellied pots are often suited with

8

decoration on the visible upper surface of the sphere. Necks, shoulders, or feet are distinctive features which may be effectively enhanced by different treatment from the rest of the surface.

Any of these treatments may be applied to the surfaces of models, and scratched textures can be descriptive of cloth, bricks and the like. Children often model on a small scale using scratching to describe important features such as eyes, noses or windows, but their work grows in expressive power if it is of a scale allowing these parts to be modelled, reserving scratching for surface textures only (Plate 23). Modelled work of this kind depends on observation which may be helped by discussion; a child may, for instance, have a rough idea of the form of a cat, but careful questioning can reveal to him that his knowledge is considerably greater than he thought. Attention should be called to fundamental features which will later appear in the model.

Similarly, observation can be sharpened by drawing which is the only satisfactory starting point for decorations other than texture or geometrical pattern. In drawing an object one needs to look not only at details, but also at the underlying structure and relationship of the parts: the casual glance at an object reveals none of these features and leaves no permanent image in the mind. Visual memory requires training, and the floral designs or animal drawings produced from memory by most inexperienced students do not often lend themselves to the creation of exciting or personal pottery designs.

Bibliography to Chapter 6

The following books are recommended comprehensive manuals of the craft containing full information about the preparation of materials; methods of making including throwing, turning and mouldmaking; glazes; kilns and firing.

Bernard Leach, A POTTER'S BOOK. *Faber and Faber.* This book is more than a manual, it is also an appreciation of the craft and has been standard reading since it first appeared in 1939. Its bias towards Oriental methods provides an interesting contrast with other manuals. It contains 80 photographs of fine pots and potters at work, and many explanatory drawings of tools, wheels and kilns.

William Ruscoe, A MANUAL FOR THE POTTER. *Tiranti (Paperback edition 1959).* Mr. Ruscoe worked in the Stoke potteries for many years and there is a bias towards industrial techniques in these pages – especially among the well produced photographs. Industrial and studio kilns are described; the line drawings in the text clearly explain other tools and hand or machine methods of making and decorating.

D. M. Billington, THE TECHNIQUE OF POTTERY. *Batsford* 1962. Readable and complete, with clear diagrams of tools and techniques, and a critical appraisal of their uses and possibilities. The techniques are also related to periods in history, and selected examples are often illustrated; the basic processes are also illustrated by sequences of photographs.

Murray Fieldhouse, POTTERY. *Foyle's Handbooks* 1952. Restricted to earthenware production and without photographs, but for the low paperback price is excellent value. Processes are explained with the aid of line drawings, and it contains plans of a kick-wheel and small coal kiln.

Kenneth Clark, PRACTICAL POTTERY AND CERAMICS. *Studio* 1964. Ninety photographs of exciting pots and design exercises, and fifty black and white drawings of tools or processes make this short book a valuable one for beginners. The examples are marked by a freedom of approach to clay and the instructions are clear. The author is a potter, business man and teacher, and the resulting combination is stimulating.

Books with an Emphasis on Work with Children

Maria Petrie, MODELLING. *Dryad Press, 7th edition 1959*. An essay on the needs and capabilities of children of all ages in terms of three-dimensional work and thinking. Though published originally in 1936, it will not be outdated. Technical information is confined to methods of casting solid clay models in plaster. 8 photographs of typical children's work.

John Newick, CLAY AND TERRACOTTA IN EDUCATION. *Dryad Press 1964*. An essay on the appreciation and techniques of terracotta modelling which is practical in its approach. Contains sections on clay forms and expression, teaching methods and kiln building. 10 plates.

Margaret P. Hall, TERRACOTTA MODELLING FOR SCHOOLS. *Tiranti 1954 (paperback)*. Short, inexpensive and recommended as a guide to methods of teaching. Diagrams are included showing how several different kinds of figure models are built, and there are directions for building and firing a small brick-built, wood-fired kiln. Contains photographs of 20 characteristic models by children.

Karl Hils, CRAFTS FOR ALL. *Routledge and Kegan Paul 1960*. An inspired book about many crafts. Only one of sixteen chapters is devoted to pottery, but this covers all that is required to start young children. There are exciting ideas in all the chapters – especially on the making of musical instruments – and the whole book is recommended.

Seonaid Robertson, BEGINNING AT THE BEGINNING WITH CLAY. Published by the Society for Education Through Art, Morley College, Westminster Bridge Road, London, S.E.1 (2/6 + postage). This illustrated pamphlet explains the methods used by a successful pottery teacher. Full of ideas and excellent value.

Other Books of Technical Interest

Daniel Rhodes, CLAY AND GLAZES FOR THE POTTER. *Pitman 1957.* A readable and exhaustive account which has become a standard reference book for studio potters and teachers. The first part deals with the geology, chemistry and firing of clays, and a section is devoted to mixing clays and bodies for all kinds of pot manufacture. Glazes are similarly explained. The book is clearly indexed, and includes 25 good photographs of historical and modern examples. Unfortunately many of the materials discussed are of American origin.

Daniel Rhodes. STONEWARE AND PORCELAIN, THE ART OF HIGH-FIRED POTTERY. *Pitman 1960.* This excellent book contains a historical appreciation of the subject as well as complete information on clays, glazes, methods of production and decoration. Over 80 good illustrations. Again the materials discussed are often of American origin.

Ernst Rosenthal, POTTERY AND CERAMICS. *Pelican 1952.* An inexpensive and comprehensive account of the full range of industrial ceramics, including tableware, bricks, refractories and insulator porcelain.

Books of General Interest

Ernst Rottger, CREATIVE CLAYCRAFT. *Batsford 1963.* A stimulating book presenting an attitude of free thinking and adventure with the material. It is divided into sections dealing with basic clay shapes (the ball, block, sheet and strip), their development into models or pots, texturing and surface ornamentation. The 250 illustrations have a fascination which could, however, be inhibiting if they were to be used as copies, or shown to students as examples whilst they were working.

POTTERY QUARTERLY. *Northfields Studio, Northfields, Tring, Herts.* An interesting periodical covering all aspects of studio pottery, and including advertisements of equipment for sale or wanted. One looks forward to each issue and any back-numbers should be sought.

Vincent Eley. A MONK AT THE POTTER'S WHEEL. *Edmund Ward.* This book is not only a useful handbook, but also the story of the development of an interesting potter and his workshop told in an entertaining way. The author's enthusiasm, and the vigour of his approach to each fresh problem, are infectious.

Marguerite Wildenhain. POTTERY FORM AND EXPRESSION. (*Enlarged edition.*) *American Craftsmen's Council. Reinhold Publishing Co., New York 1962.* This book contains information about methods and techniques, but its aim is to enhance the readers' appreciation and manipulation of clay forms and surfaces, and to broaden their general understanding of creative work. It is lavishly illustrated with splendid photographs of historical examples and students' work. The author was educated at the Bauhaus and taught there for a time.

W. Fishley Holland, FIFTY YEARS A POTTER. *Pottery Quarterly 1958*. This book pictures a different side of pottery from that which is described by Rosenthal, Eley or Leach. It is the story of country potteries in North Devon producing common domestic articles. Fishley Holland was a master potter who owned and ran his own business with success.

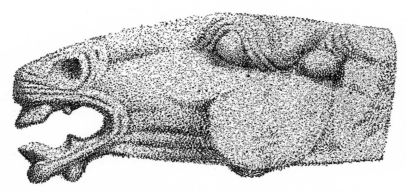

Head of a horse; the result of a combination of observation, visual memory and a sure sense of sculptural form. Chinese, 220–589 A.D.

Chapter 7

Glazes and Glazing

In the past potters have been secretive about glazes and their silence has created a mystical atmosphere which, to the mind of the layman, is often encouraged by a glance at some recipes or formulae. Are glaze ingredients really so mysterious, and is their chemistry so incomprehensible? Is it not possible for anyone to produce their own recipes, and to prospect for some of their own raw materials?

Plate 11 shows a soft brick broken into two pieces, one of which was refired at 1300° C. The high temperature almost melted this piece causing it to glassify, and Plate 12 of some molten clay that has accidentally become runny enough to creep inside a kiln element, where it suffered extreme heat, shows the completion of the process – it has been turned into brown glass. Perhaps an investigation into the ingredients of glazes could start at this point: different clays obviously vary in their melting points because the clay inside the element wire was not at a temperature above 1100° C. when it first became runny enough to get inside the coils, and there were many other pots in the same kiln which had not started to soften, or go out of shape, at this temperature.

GLAZES

On page 74 it was stated that most clay is descended from felspar and that the pure material – china clay or kaolin – melts at about 1800° C. Pure clay is a compound of aluminium oxide (known as alumina, Al_2O_3), silicon dioxide (silica SiO_2) and water which is driven off when the material is heated above 500° C. As the melting point of alumina is 2050° C. and silica 1713° C. one can only assume that, when compounded together, some reaction takes place causing the lowering of the melting point of alumina by some 250° and raising that of silica by nearly 100°.

Though the proportion of alumina to silica varies from one clay to another it would seem doubtful, however, that this reaction can ever be strong enough to lower the melting point of a clay sufficiently to cause it to glassify at pottery glaze temperatures. If proof is sought, a proportion of alumina to silica such as is found in an average low temperature clay (one of alumina to three of silica) could be tested by firing. The statement on page 74 concludes by saying that *impure* varieties of clay sometimes melt at only a little over half the temperature required by china clay, so that it may be pertinent at this point to discover precisely what impurities are usually found in clays. The following table shows that all natural clays contain varying amounts of potassium oxide (potash, K_2O), sodium oxide (soda, Na_2O), iron oxide (Fe_2O_3), magnesium oxide (magnesia, MgO) and calcium oxide (lime, CaO), as well as small amounts of other substances.

	Basic Ingredients		'Impurities'				
	Al_2O_3	SiO_2	K_2O	Na_2O	Fe_2O_3	MgO	CaO
Theoretical Pure Clay	39·3	46·1					
China Clay	37·7	46·3	0·9	0·7	0·3	0·1	0·8
Dorset Ball Clay	27·9	58·4	2·6	0·4	1·1	0·2	0·4
Devon Stoneware Clay	24·7	63·6	2·3	0·3	0·8	0·4	0·4
Red Clay	21·9	59·6	0·8	0·8	6·6	0·8	0·6
Fire Clay (Siliceous)	18·7	68·7	1·0	0·1	2·4	0·3	0·2

These figures are in percentages, but minute amounts of other oxides, and between 7 and 14% of combustible material—mostly water—have not been shown.

As might be expected these 'impurities' are all among the common rock-forming oxides to be found in the Earth, and some tests may well be carried out by adding different amounts of these oxides to china clay. Firing temperatures will affect the results.*

From the results of these tests it will be appreciated that these oxides do in fact have some 'fluxing' effect on the china clay, though the results may not be entirely satisfactory

* For effective testing the powders need to be reasonably well mixed together and evenly spread so that it is best to weigh them into a pestle and mortar and grind for a moment or two with sufficient water to produce a cream. This fluid mix is then spread evenly round the interior of a biscuit-fired clay bowl by pouring it in and emptying after a lapse of about five seconds. The oxides themselves, with the exception of iron, react strongly with water so that potters use the more stable carbonate forms making allowance for the amount of carbon dioxide which will be driven away during the firing. The oxide content of the carbonates is 58·1% for potassium, 58·5% for sodium, 47·8% for magnesium and 56% for calcium, so that between 40% and 50% more carbonate has to be used to incorporate the required amount of oxide.

glazes. At 1100° C. some of the mixtures may be partially fused, whilst others are still almost powdery even when refired at 1300° C. It will be seen immediately that iron oxide is a strong colourant which, though it may be partially effective as a flux, must be rejected at once as a basic glaze ingredient.

The reader is probably aware that white sand – almost pure silica – is the basic ingredient of glass, and may be surprised that clay should occupy this position in pottery glazes. There are three reasons for this; firstly the potter does not melt his silica and other ingredients in a pot and use them whilst they are cooling, he applies them as powders to his pot and requires them to be viscous enough when molten to adhere to vertical surfaces. The proportion of alumina in clay provides this stability and enables a glaze to mature slowly over a considerable range of temperature without becoming too runny. Secondly, as has already been noted, alumina on its own is a rare substance confined to only a few districts of the world in the form of bauxite ore so that the high proportion contained in clay is welcome. Thirdly the sticky nature of clay serves to bind the dry powdery ingredients to the surface of the pot so that they do not flake or dust off before firing.

The four oxides apart from iron – potash, soda, magnesia and lime are all known as fluxes. They vary in their activity and have different effects on surface qualities and colours. Glazes are often classified by their predominant flux hence 'lime matt', 'soda', 'alkaline' (potash and soda). Several other metallic oxides (boron, zinc, barium, lithium, strontium) have similar fluxing action on silica and, though they are not common oxides, they may occasionally be used to obtain some special effect. Lead oxide is exceptional and is certainly the most effective fluxing agent at low temperatures, though its use declines rapidly above 1200° C. Lead oxide is highly poisonous in *all* forms, but some pre-fused mixtures of lead and silica are considered safe enough for use in schools.* Proportions of these lead silicates with various pottery clays – especially red clays – will quickly yield attractive earthenware glazes like those used in Europe for many centuries, and the recipes may be discovered by the use of a simple line blend technique:†

Lead silicate‡	100	90	80	70	60	50	40	30	20	10	
Any clay		10	20	30	40	50	60	70	80	90	100

(additions of 5%–10% of extra silica (flint) may also be tried)

Three other types of glazes were mentioned in Chapter 3 which readers may like to

---

* Lead bisilicate contains 35 % silica, 65 % lead; lead sesquisilicate contains 28 % silica, 72 % lead.
  † The line blend is a useful means of testing combinations of two materials, but in this example only those pairs shown in ordinary type are likely to yield results. The method is often used for colour trials.
  ‡ Leadless boracic glazes may also be evolved by substituting a borax frit (borax, being soluble, cannot be used on its own) in place of the lead silicate.

experiment with; these are ash, salt and Oriental felspathic glazes. All three are dependent upon high temperatures (1200° C.–1300° C.), and are generally associated with reduction firing, though this is not essential.

All vegetable matter is composed largely of hydrogen and carbon compounds, but when these have been burned away a small deposit is left of non-combustible material which consists mainly of the six chief 'ceramic' oxides (alumina, silica, lime, soda, magnesia and potash) with the fluxes strongly predominating. Ash compositions vary from one tree to another, or one plant to another, from season to season, and from district to district, so that rich variety can be expected from glazes of which they form a part. Ashes are prepared for use by soaking in water and sieving (anything from 40-mesh to 120 depending on smoothness of required result) to remove coarse or unburned particles. When dried some line blends can be tested with various clays and the resulting mixtures can be applied to damp, unbiscuited, pots like a coating of slip (raw glazing).

| Any ash | | 90 | 80 | 70 | 60 | 50 | | | | |
| Any clay | | 10 | 20 | 30 | 40 | 50 | | | | |

Salt-glazing is also carried out on unbiscuited ware, but the substance is not applied direct to the pots, it is thrown into the fire when the temperature has reached about 1200° C., and after a period of reduction firing. About half a pound of common salt is required per cubic foot of kiln space. Plain salt-glaze on grey or 'buff' stoneware clays produces only shades of brown, but a wide range of colour and texture can be produced by applying other glazes or slips to the pots first. *Salt-glazing produces poisonous fumes of chlorine and hydrochloric acid, and should therefore only be tried in kilns built out of doors in fairly open surroundings. Under no circumstances should it be tried in electric kilns.*

Felspathic glazes are based on rocks (orthoclase or potassium felspar, albite or soda felspar, anorthite or lime felspar, nepheline syenite and Cornish stone) which have similar compositions to the clay which is derived from them. The chemical equation on page 73 shows that felspars (in this case orthoclase) contain a proportion of flux, and some varieties of felspar can in fact serve as glazes at high pottery temperatures (1250°–1300° C.). Some additions of flux and silica are usually made, however, to adjust the fitting of the glaze to the clay of the pot, and to reduce the occurrence of blemishes.

The additions are usually made in the forms of limestone or whiting (both calcium carbonate), and flint or quartz (both silica). Felspathic recipes are often further complicated by the addition of more clay to improve the handling qualities of the glaze before firing.

More variety can also be obtained from ashes by incorporating them into felspathic compositions, and the following tests, especially when considered with the addition of colouring oxides (see page 127) and reduction firing, lead directly to many of the subtle stoneware and porcelain colours of the Far East.

Any ash			70	60	50	40	30			
Any igneous rock			30	40	50	60	70			

Any ash			50	45	40	35		
Any predominantly felspathic rock			30	35	40	45		
Any clay			20	20	20	20		

(The clay content may also be varied)

Felspathic rock	100	80	70	50(3)	40						
Flint or quartz (silica)			10	33(2)	30						
Limestone, whiting or any other form of calcium carbonate		20	20	17(1)	20						
Any clay				10							

Felspars are associated with granite and other igneous rocks, and it will be found that the compositions of these are also sometimes suitable for making high temperature glazes without many additions (see table on page 125). Igneous rocks are not used in the industry because of their variability and their iron content, but many interesting surfaces or colours may be discovered by substituting them for the mineral felspar in the last line of tests listed above (Plate 20). Readers may be daunted by the thought of powdering granite or basalt, but these rocks – and others – are often used by stonemasons, whose polishing and sawing machines yield quantities of sludge of almost ceramic fineness which they are generally only too willing to give away. The sludge requires only sieving and drying before use.

It will be evident that the provision of roughly glassified coatings on pottery is a simple matter and some enjoyable texture or colour may well be discovered from the experiments. However, finding a glaze that *never* crazes, *never* has little holes in it, or crawls up in lumps – or even flakes off altogether – is an entirely different matter. Glazes have to be suited to the clay of the pot in terms of equivalent shrinkage and, when found, will need standardized firing schedules and temperatures. In industry much of this control is effected by analysis and calculation based not on weights or percentages, but on numbers and proportions of molecules. The recipes on page 124 are also shown in this form.

Most studio potters rely upon rule of thumb methods or experience, and help will be found in the books listed in the bibliography. So far as the trials indicated in this chapter are concerned, it should suffice to watch fusibility; glazes containing too much flux flow down the sides of pots and collect as pools in the bottom of bowls (to avoid damage to kiln shelves *all* mixtures or substances being tested for the first time should be applied to the interior of bowls only) and glazes with too little flux appear dry to the touch, or they may be blistered or pinholed.

The flux content can easily be altered, but an alteration of the firing temperature may be equally effective; a mixture that is too runny at 1300° C. may be excellent at 1100° C. or 1200° C. Similarly a dry feel, or pinholing, may be the result of under-firing; a glaze that appears like a dead coat of plaster at 1100° C. may be gloriously translucent at stoneware heat. Excessive gloss – especially in lead glazes – may be dulled by the addition of up to 10 or 15 % of extra clay which increases the proportion of alumina.

PREPARING AND APPLYING GLAZES

Mixing a glaze from a recipe using prepared raw materials supplied by a potter's merchant is an easy job. The powders are weighed and then stirred into sufficient water to provide a creamy mixture which is brushed through a '120' sieve or lawn. Plastic buckets with lids are ideal containers, and they can hold between 3000 and 4000 grams of dry glaze powder with the appropriate amount of water. Smaller quantities – except of course for testing purposes – are not really useful.

After the glaze has been sieved the water content will probably need adjusting. If the biscuit ware, red, grey or white clay, is fired at 1050° C., then most glazes need to be creamy enough to just coat a dry finger. However, some glazes give their best results when applied thickly, others when thin, and the most suitable coating can only be found by experience. In general, matt or opaque glazes need to be applied thickly, whilst transparent ones – especially commercial earthenware glazes – are better thinly applied. Thickness of coating also depends on the length of time the pot is held within the glaze which adheres because the porous biscuit absorbs water from the mixture leaving a layer of the powdered ingredients on the surface. If the pot is immersed too long the clay becomes saturated and little powder is retained on the surface. Soluble substances cannot be used directly in glazes because they upset this simple absorption process.

The best method of applying glazes is by dipping the pots into the mixtures and small quantities are irritating because they do not cover even minute articles. Glazes in use need stirring continuously, especially those containing heavy lead compounds, and it is advisable to stir occasionally between times otherwise the powdery ingredients settle to a solid mass which is hard to remix. Replacing 2 or 3 % of clay in the recipe by the same amount of bentonite stops settling to some extent.

When there is not enough glaze to cover an article by dipping the next best method is to

Recipes and Molecular Formulae of Glazes

| | RECIPES | | | MOLECULAR FORMULAE | | | | | | |
	Raw Material	%	K₂O	CaO	MgO	PbO	BaO	Al₂O₃	SiO₂
A 1080°– 1100°C	Lead bisilicate Whiting Felspar China clay	56·7 5·5 30·6 7·1	0·2	0·2	—	0·6	—	0·3	2·6
B 1080°– 1100°C	Lead bisilicate Cornish stone China clay Flint	72·7 13·4 12·1 1·6	0·1	—	—	0·9	—	0·3	3·0
C 1200°C	Felspar Whiting Lead bisilicate China clay Flint	35·5 10·5 46·6 4·0 5·4	0·2	0·35	—	0·45	—	0·25	2·5
D 1200°C	Felspar Whiting Barium carbonate China clay Flint	37·8 13·5 26·6 13·1 9·0	0·2	0·4	—	—	0·4	0·35	1·94
E 1280°– 1300°C	Felspar China clay Whiting Flint	37 11 15 37	0·3	0·7	—	—	—	0·51	5·1
F 1280°– 1300°C	Felspar Dolomite China clay Whiting Flint	35·2 4·7 27·2 20·3 12·2	0·2	0·7	0·1	—	—	0·53	2·5

		K_2O	Na_2O	CaO	MgO	Al_2O_3	SiO_2	Other oxides	Loss on heating
GLAZES									
1100°C {	A	5·3	—	5·3	—	7·7	66·8	PbO 14·9	—
	B	2·0	—	—	—	6·6	70·2	PbO 21·2	—
1200°C {	C	6·0	—	6·2	—	8·1	47·9	PbO 13·8	—
	D	7·4	—	8·8	BaO 24·0	14	45·8	—	—
1300°C {	E	4·7	—	10·6	—	7·7	77·0	—	—
	F	4·9	—	17·9	2·1	13·3	62·0	—	—
RAW MATERIALS									
Potash felspar		11·1	2·5	0·2	0·1	19·4	66·0	Fe_2O_3 0·05	0·2
Soda felspar		—	9·1	0·8	—	20·5	67·2	Fe_2O_3 0·1	2·1
Cornish stone		4·6	2·0	0·9	0·1	18·6	70·3	Fe_2O_3 0·3	3·0
Keswick granite		2·5	2·0	2·3	1·3	15·7	68·3	Fe_2O_3 4·8	2·6
Charnwood granite		3·8	1·0	6·3	4·1	16·1	61·3	Fe_2O_3 7·2	—
Basalt		1·5	3·2	8·9	6·2	15·7	49·1	Fe_2O_3 11·7	1·6
Apple ash		0·9	—	54	3·3	2·0	2·7	Fe_2O_3 2·4	34·7
Nepheline syenite		5·2	10·5	0·4	—	23·3	60·1	0·1	0·4

EXPERIMENTS FOR RAKU GLAZES (750° – 900° C.).

		*	*	
Red or white lead	80	70	60	50
Flint	20	30	40	50
Borax (increasing as lead decreases)			10	20
China clay for stability	2 – 5%			

* These mixtures are similar to lead bi- or sesquisilicates see page 120.

pour the glaze over it. Provided the glaze is poured in a good stream – not slowly dribbled – this works very well. Cup shapes are filled to the brim with glaze which is poured out straight away, they are then held upside down and glaze is poured over the outside. If there is more than a moment or two of time lag between glazing the inside and the outside the moisture from the inner glaze will have time to seep through to the exterior surface of the pot which will then be too wet to absorb a proper coat. Narrow-necked or tall vases should not be filled; a little glaze is poured inside which is then slowly tipped out whilst the pot is being rotated. If tall pots are filled they cannot be emptied quickly enough and too thick a coating adheres to the walls.

Very flat shapes can be rested on edge on sticks placed over a bowl, and be held upright by one finger. The stream of glaze from a jug is then split over the rim so that back and front are glazed at once.

The chief difficulty with both pouring and dipping is how to hold the pot so that as few finger marks as possible are left on the glazed surface. Most models have bases which can be held quite easily, but many pot forms are difficult unless the problem has been carefully thought out in the shaping. Bowl shapes, or cylindrical forms that have no emphasis or change of form at the bottom, are difficult to glaze, but they can be stood upside down on sticks across a bucket as was suggested for flat dishes. The stick marks on the rim can be touched up, but this has to be done carefully when using opaque or matt glazes. A pair of tongs with sharpened points may be useful.

Touching up stick or finger marks is done with a brush and, when dry, the marks are carefully scraped to the level of the glaze film with a razor blade or other sharp-edged piece of metal. If the fingers are liberally coated with glaze beforehand touching up is made easier, but the business should be avoided wherever possible by designing graspable feet or other areas which can be left unglazed.

Glazes can be sprayed on to biscuit ware, but compressors and spray guns are expensive and *must* be used in conjunction with a proper booth and extractor fan. Spraying is only used in industry on difficult decorated wares or large cumbersome objects such as sinks or toilets. The occasional model or pot which cannot be dealt with by any other method can fairly successfully be painted. A few spots of gum arabic or tragacanth mixed in with the glaze make it easier to use this way, and several coats applied with a soft flat brush in different directions will be required.

Transparent glazes depend for their effect on the colour of the clay of the pot or the colours of slips which have been applied to it, but other colours of glaze can easily be achieved by mixing a small proportion of certain metallic oxides – or carbonates – with the glazes. On the next page is a list of the effective colouring oxides together with the average proportions in which they are added to glazes.*

* These oxides have been listed in the order in which they appear in the Periodic Table of the Elements, and it is interesting to note that they occur together.

Oxide	Range of addition	Colour
Vanadium oxide	2–10%	gives yellows
Chromium oxide	1–5%	greens, pink in tin glazes
Manganese oxide	2–9%	purple–brown
Iron oxide	$\frac{1}{2}$–10%	browns–black, celedon when reduced
Cobalt oxide	$\frac{1}{8}$–1%	blues
Nickel oxide	1–3%	greys
Copper oxide	1–6%	greens, purples or reds when reduced

Colouring oxides can of course be combined and an infinite number of colours obtained from them which will also be affected to some extent by the fluxing oxides. The range of colour available in transparent glazes over red clay is limited, but white slip can be applied to the red clay first or the glaze itself may be opacified to cover up the strong brown colour. Opaque glazes are useful; transparent earthenware glazes can be made opaque by the addition of tin oxide in the proportion of between 8% and 10% as were the glazes on faience, delft or maiolica.

Temperature also has an effect on colour. Above 1100° C. the clay and glaze layers become increasingly united, and the one influences the other; the high proportion of iron in red clay makes it impossible to achieve any other colour than brown, but red clay pots fired at a high temperature may have very pleasant surface qualities. Iron is by far the most important colorant at stoneware temperatures, but its most pleasing attributes can only be obtained in what is known as 'reduction' firings which are not advisable in electric kilns because they shorten the life of the heating elements. For part of the duration of a reduced firing the interior atmosphere of the kiln is deprived of enough oxygen to burn the fuel properly, and it is therefore saturated with hot carbon and hydrogen gases which attack the ferric oxide (Fe_2O_3) content of clays and glazes reducing it to ferrous oxide (FeO). All the other ceramic oxides except copper and lead are stable enough to withstand the attack. Similar effects cannot be obtained by using ferrous oxide in glazes in the first place because, in an ordinary firing, it will straight away acquire more oxygen.

The reader will doubtless enjoy experimenting with these colours in the glazes produced from the experiments or those on page 124 including the Raku ones. However, it is important to have some results from clay work as soon as a kiln becomes available and for this reason it would be advisable to purchase one or two ready-made and tested glazes from the merchants. In busy pottery studios or departments the run-of-the-mill glazes, such as transparent earthenware, are usually provided from this source as there is little chance of producing better mixtures oneself, and some time can be saved. Low-solubility lead glazes are acceptable in schools and are much easier to handle than the leadless ones which are sometimes advertised for school use.

Bibliography to Chapter 7

Chapters in general handbooks:

Bernard Leach, A POTTER'S BOOK.

William Ruscoe, A MANUAL FOR THE POTTER.

D. M. Billington, THE TECHNIQUE OF POTTERY.

Vincent Eley, A MONK AT THE POTTER'S WHEEL.

Discussion in greater detail:

Daniel Rhodes, CLAY AND GLAZES FOR THE POTTER.

Daniel Rhodes, STONEWARE AND PORCELAIN.

(For details of the above books see bibliography to Chapter 6, pages 114 to 117.)

David Green, UNDERSTANDING POTTERY GLAZES. *Faber and Faber 1963.* This book covers in outline the chemistry of glazes, the geology of raw materials, calculations including use of slide rules, colouring, opacifying and correction of flaws. It contains 22 photographs and 11 tables of analyses of materials.

Pyrometric Cones and Temperature Correlations

British Cones	American Orton Cones	Temperature °C.	Temperature °F.	Colour Visible in Kiln Interior	Processes and Reactions
	018	720	1328	Red heat begins to show at 600°C. after which point the colour steadily increases in brilliance	
017		730	1346		
016		750	1382		Enamel or on-glaze colours
	017	770	1418		
015*		790	1454		
	016	795	1463		
	015	805	1481		
014*		815	1499		
	014	830	1526		
013*		835	1535		
012*		855	1571		
	013	860	1580		
	012	875	1607		

British Cones	American Orton Cones	Temperature °C.	Temperature °F.	Colour Visible in Kiln Interior	Processes and Reactions
011*		880	1616		
	011	895	1643		
010*		900	1652		
	010	905	1661		
09*		920	1688		
	09	930	1706		
08*		940	1724		
	08	950	1742		
07*		960	1760		
06*		980	1796		Soft lead glazes sometimes opacified with tin oxide
	07	990	1814		
05*		1000	1832	Bright cherry-red	
	06	1015	1859		
04*		1020	1868		
03*	05	1040	1904		Porous biscuit
02*	04	1060	1940	Redness begins to turn to orange	Earthenware and bone china glaze
01*		1080	1976		
1*		1100	2012		
	03	1115	2039		
2*		1120	2048		
	02	1125	2057		
3*		1140	2084		

British Cones	American Orton Cones	Temperature °C.	Temperature °F.	Colour Visible in Kiln Interior	Processes and Reactions
	01	1145	2093	Brilliant light orange	Industrial earthenware biscuit (virtually non-porous)
4*	1	1160	2120		
	2	1165	2129		
	3	1170	2138		
5*		1180	2156		
	4	1190	2174		
6*		1200	2192	Orange colour begins to give way to white	Some stonewares and salt-glaze
	5	1205	2201		
7	6	1230	2246		
8	7	1250	2282		
	8	1260	2300	Distinctly white colour changing to intense white at 1350°C. and showing signs of blueness at 1450°C.	Usual stoneware temperature. Bone china biscuit
9		1280	2336		
	9	1285	2345		
10		1300	2372		
	10	1305	2381		Some porcelains, others up to 1450°C.
11		1320	2408		
	11	1325	2417		

* British Cones marked with an asterisk sometimes have a letter A after the number, thus 013A or 5A. From some suppliers all the numbers are preceded by a letter H.

Equipment, Materials and Suppliers

The following list shows the equipment and raw materials required to embark on work and experiments along the lines suggested in this book. The quantities of raw materials are minimal, they would go a long way with one person, but in a school they would only last a short time, though long enough for the teacher to decide which suit him best. Quantities of small tools are suggested for classes of about a dozen children.

The firms listed are those whose products and service are known to the author; there are many others, possibly some nearer to the reader, who doubtless are equally good and whose addresses may be found from advertisements in *Pottery Quarterly* (see page 116). Most of the following small tools and raw materials may be purchased from Podmore & Sons Ltd. and Wengers Ltd., and where no other supplier is mentioned it may be presumed that the item is available from both these firms. Considerable saving can be made in packing and transport charges by giving a comprehensive order to one firm; some suppliers encourage this by increasing their prices on small orders.

N.B. Addresses of all the firms mentioned are listed at the end.

Kilns

The following firms supply electric kilns suitable for use in schools, together with pyrometers, etc.:

The Applied Heat Co. Ltd., British Ceramic Services Co. Ltd., Cromartie Kilns Ltd., Catterson-Smith, Bernard W. E. Webber, Kilns & Furnaces Ltd., Podmore & Sons Ltd., Wengers Ltd.

Kiln Building Materials

Local builders' merchants supply firebricks of various thicknesses, 9 inches by $4\frac{1}{2}$ inches by 3, $2\frac{1}{2}$, 2 or 1 inch, common bricks and fireclay. Local ironfounders will make firebars to fill the measurements of your grate. New materials are expensive; a gas works may be able to supply used firebricks of good quality, and commons may be found anywhere though there may be a lot of cleaning to do with mash hammer and cold chisel or bricklayer's hammer. The following firms supplied specialized materials for the kilns illustrated:

Allen & Sons Ltd., SELFRAC REFRACTORY INSULATION BRICKS.

John G. Stein & Co. Ltd., No. 13 CASTABLE REFRACTORY CONCRETE.

White Bros. (Iron-founders) Ltd., FIREBARS.

For list of suppliers all round the country see a copy of the *Refractories Journal*, London & Sheffield Publishing Co. Ltd., 7, Chesterfield Gardens, Curzon Street, London, W.1.

Podmore's now offer refractory bricks and cements in small quantities.

The Lafarge Aluminous Cement Co. Ltd., will send list of suppliers of Ciment Fondu and suitable aggregates. Suppliers in every district.

Kiln Shelves and Supports

Acme Marls Ltd.

Kiln shelves seem naturally to be accident-prone, so it is useful to have a few in stock. Order sizes as near as possible to the full area of the kiln floor (about half a dozen) unless it is over 18 inches square; half area (6 or 8) and quarter area (one dozen). Stipulate high temperature always (H.T.).

N.B. One inch must always be left clear between the shelves and the kiln wall to allow heat to circulate. This gap should be greater with flame-producing kilns.

Plain tile cranks, 9 inches by 6 inches (1 or 2 dozen). Plain rectangular dots. No. 3 (1 or 2 gross).
Interlocking prop system G. 175. One gross 1 inch (H.T.), one gross $1\frac{1}{2}$ inch (H.T.). Two dozen height-adjusting fittings, G. 175 S.T. (H.T.).
Stilts for glazed ware from Podmore or Wengers (one gross each of Nos. oz, 1 and 2).

Pyrometric Cones

If a pyrometer is fitted to the kiln these are not necessary, but to test accuracy of the instrument order 1 dozen each of Nos. 3, 03A (1040° C., biscuit), 1A (1100° C., earthenware glaze), 9 (1280° C., usual stoneware finish).

Without pyrometer buy the following numbers so that the progress of temperature rise can be observed:

05A (1000° C.), 03A (1040° C.), 01A (1080° C.), 1A (1100° C.), 5A (1180° C.), 6 (1200° C.), 7 (1230° C.), 8 (1250° C.), 9 (1280° C.), 10 (1300° C.).

The letter A is omitted from Podmore's list.

Concrete Clay Preparation Slab

Ideally this should be built on brick piers, and the space underneath could be fitted with metal-lined doors, shelves and a water trough on the floor, to act as a clay store. Height needs to be between 30 and 36 inches, and the surface area as long as possible but at least 2 feet deep. The builder will skim the top of the concrete with a cement mix giving a smooth surface, but if this mix contains too high a proportion of cement it will not be sufficiently porous and clay will tend to stick (Plate 13).

If the floor of the studio is wooden 2 or 3 inches of concrete can be laid on one or more substantial tables.

Plaster Drying Slab

A thick plaster slab in wooden frame, about 18 inches to 24 inches square, is useful for drying clay. Use dental plaster (local builders' merchant).

Workbenches

Clay working benches should have wood or linoleum tops giving a little absorbency. Tops of glazing benches should be of zinc or plastic laminate.

Clay

If adequate storage is available try one or two hundredweight of each of the following:

Red clay, Potclay's Crank Mixture and St. Thomas' Body, Podmore's B.34 and B.32, and Moira Pottery Co., Ltd. Stoneware Modelling clay. (This latter is cheap and has the possible advantage of rapid delivery.) Also fireclay in powder form from a local builders' merchant, or Wengers and Podmores.

Small Tools

Some form of turntable is useful for shaping or decorating round pots or dishes so that where throwing wheels are not available buy a BANDING WHEEL or WHIRLER, the heavier the better. Wengers sell a 12-inch diameter 'Heavy Whirler' and an 8-inch 'Bench Whirler'. One of each would be useful if the money is available.

At least three HOOPED IRON WIRE CUTTERS will be required giving different thicknesses of clay sheet (1 inch, $\frac{5}{8}$ inch, $\frac{3}{8}$ inch) and having a clearance between prongs of about 18 inches. These are easy to make; use $\frac{1}{4}$ inch or $\frac{3}{8}$ inch square sectioned metal rod, bend in a vice and saw off accurately. File saw cuts smooth, then measure correct distances back and drill two small holes to take a piece of piano wire (also local ironmongers). The wire needs to be under some tension. At the same time also make one or two hand-sized cutters of lighter metal rod and brass snare wire (overall dimensions about 4 inches square) for trimming edges of moulded dishes.

Six CLAY CUTTING NEEDLES in wooden handles. Never allow ordinary sewing needles to be used, they are lost too easily in the clay.

Two wooden ROLLING PINS, as large as possible. China rolling pins stick to clay.

Two POTTERS' FETTLING KNIVES. (Wengers 3014W.) These need sharpening, as all knives do, when first purchased.

Six varied sizes and shapes of BLUED STEEL SCRAPERS or PALETTES (Wengers 4017W–4020W, Podmore's PE 25 and 26).

Four RUBBER KIDNEYS for smoothing clay slabs and moulded dishes – use in conjunction with sponge and a little water. (Wengers 4013–6W, Podmore's PE 40–42).

Twelve STANLEY No. 493B SURFORM CUTTING BLADES. These are useful for shaping any leather-hard clay and, as they have wide slotted teeth, are the only pattern that does not clog. Coarse clays wear them out rather quickly (local tool shop).

HACKSAW BLADES and any other saw blades having varied teeth for scraping and decorating (local tool shop).

Six NATURAL SPONGES (Wengers 4003W, Podmore's PE 27).

Six SYNTHETIC BENCH SPONGES for cleaning (Podmore's PE 29).

Three 4-inch flat PAINT SCRAPERS for cleaning benches and cutting up scrap clay. Buy only those with tempered steel blades fitted right through the handle; the cheap ones break easily. (Harris Brush Co. produce an excellent rustless one with plastic handle and hole to hang it up by. Available at local paint suppliers.)

One sheet 8 ft. × 4 ft. × $\frac{1}{4}$ in. ASBESTOS (local builders' merchant). Quite the best board for clay sheet, etc., as its absorbency prevents sticking and aids drying. Cut the asbestos sheet, or score it with an old chisel and snap, into 2-ft. squares, and then reduce about half of these into 12-inch and 6-inch squares. Scraps of wood of a kind which does not warp and glazed tiles are also useful for modelling on.

Selection of boxwood MODELLING TOOLS, French pattern from Tiranti (9 No. 6, 7 inches long; 3 No 3, 8 inches long; one of each 12 inches long). Also from the same firm, WIRE ENDED MODELLING TOOLS, No. 8, 7 inches long, and 4 FLAT WIRE TURNING TOOLS (2 square, 2 round) for hollowing or decorating models and pots.

One CARBORUNDUM RUBBING BLOCK for grinding shelves and the bottoms of pots. (Wengers 4040W – medium, or scythe-sharpening stones from local tool supplier.

Equipment for Preparing Slips and Glazes

One moderate-sized (9 inch) PESTLE AND MORTAR for grinding raw ingredients. A small one (6-inch) is also useful for tests and colours.

Three LAWNS or SIEVES. One 10-inch, 20 mesh, for coarse materials, ashes, etc. One 8-inch, 60-mesh for slips and glazes; one 8-inch, 120-mesh, for glazes.

Two or more 24-inch lengths of TRIANGULAR WOOD to act as supports for sieves over bucket, or for supporting pots over buckets whilst glazing.

Two SLIP BRUSHES for brushing clays and coarse materials through sieves (Wengers W.B.2). Never use sticks or spatulas for this job.

Two LAWN BRUSHES for brushing glazes and finer materials through sieves (Wengers W.B.1). Also useful for decorating.

Two ENAMEL JUGS, 4-pint and 2-pint, for glazes or slips (local supplier). Make sure they have pointed spouts and are good pourers. Flexible jugs are useless.

Various sizes of rigid POLYTHENE BOWLS. About half a dozen in all, including one large one.

At least six PLASTIC or RUBBER BUCKETS with LIDS. Rigid ones only, preferably with wire handles. More will always be useful for soaking clays and additional glazes.

One all-purpose set of SCALES. Counter-balance type without springs or weights is the most useful. The pans of laboratory balances do not hold enough to be useful in pottery. (Griffin & George Ltd., S13 – 104; 0.1 gm. to 1110 gms. or A. Gallenkamp & Co. Ltd., Rotating Weight Metric Balance, BC 161.)

Four rubber bulb SLIP TRAILERS (Wengers 4027/8W, Podmore's PE16 – or polythene PE 88), for decoration.

Three GOAT HAIR MOPS (Wengers W.B. 6, Podmore's PT 53).

Two ORIENTAL CALLIGRAPHIC BRUSHES (Wengers W.J.B. 6 and 7).

Also SCISSORS, RULERS, T-SQUARE (inexpensive), GARDEN SPRAY, SPATULAS, PALETTE KNIVES.

GUM LABELS coated with SELLOTAPE make serviceable, washable labels on polythene or glass containers.

Glaze and Slip Ingredients

Potash Felspar	.. 14 lb	Dolomite ..	..	.. 3 lb
Soda Felspar	.. 7 lb	Ball Clay ..	..	.. 14 lb
Cornish Stone	.. 14 lb	Lead Bisilicate (frit)		.. 7 lb
Nepheline Syenite	.. 7 lb	Borax frit	..	.. 7 lb
Flint	.. 14 lb	Bentonite ..	..	.. 3 lb
Whiting ..	.. 14 lb	Red Clay Powder		.. 14 lb
China Clay (powdered)	.. 14 lb	Grey Clay Powder		.. 14 lb

White Clay Powder	..	14 lb	Cobalt Oxide (black)	..	1 lb
Sodium Carbonate	..	1 lb	Copper Oxide (black)	..	1 lb
Alumina (calcined)	..	1 lb	Manganese Oxide	..	1 lb
Potassium Carbonate	..	1 lb	Iron Oxide (red) ..	..	2 lb
Magnesium Carbonate	..	1 lb	Tin Oxide ..	..	1 lb

Addresses of British Suppliers

Acme Marls Ltd.,
  Clough Street, Hanley, Stoke-on-Trent.
Allen & Sons Ltd.,
  Halifax, Yorks.
Applied Heat Co. Ltd.,
  Elecfurn Works, Otterspool Way, Watford By-Pass, Watford, Herts.
British Ceramic Services Co. Ltd.,
  Bricesco House, Wolstanton, Newcastle-under-Lyme, Staffs.
Catterson-Smith, R. M., Ltd.,
  Adam Bridge Works, South Way, Exhibition Grounds, Wembley, Middx.
Cromartie Kilns Ltd.,
  Dividy Road, Longton, Stoke-on-Trent.
Gallenkamp, A., & Co. Ltd.,
  Technico House, Christopher Street, London, E.C.2.
Griffin & George Ltd.,
  Ealing Road, Alperton, Wembley.
Kilns & Furnaces Ltd.,
  Keele Street Works, Tunstall, Stoke-on-Trent.
Lafarge Aluminous Cement Co. Ltd.,
  73, Brook Street, London, W.1.
Moira Pottery Co. Ltd.,

l materials),

Pottery: Materials and Techniques, page 137
The Nottingham Handcraft Company no longer supplies
pottery materials

Stein, John G., & Co. Ltd.,
  Bonnybridge, Scotland.
Tiranti, Alec, Ltd. (Books and sculptor's tool specialists),
  72, Charlotte Street, London, W. 1.

Webber, Bernard W. E., (S-o-T) Ltd.,
  Webcot Works, Alfred Street, Fenton, Stoke-on-Trent.
Wengers Ltd.,
  Etruria, Stoke-on-Trent.
White Bros (Ironfounders) Ltd.,
  Willow Holme, Carlisle, Cumberland.

American Suppliers

The Research and Education Department of the American Craftsmen's Council (29 West 53rd Street, New York, N.Y.) publishes a general list of craft suppliers which contains a comprehensive section on ceramics. The Council also publishes an excellent magazine, *Craft Horizons*, which is available in the United States (from the Council) and in Britain (from Alec Tiranti Limited) and is recommended.

Greek perfume bottle, 650–625 B.C.

Index

and Glossary of Ceramic Materials, Processes and Colloquial Terms

---

A

Acid. In chemistry substances are divided into two fundamental groups – acids and bases – and reactions only take place when one of each kind is present. In general the metals form 'basic' oxides and the non-metals form 'acid' ones. The chief acids in pottery are silica and boric oxide; glazes are the results of reaction between these and one or more metallic oxides.

Acid solutions, *in clay formation, 72–3*

Adobe. Sun dried mud or bricks.

Africa, *firing methods, 55*

Agate ware. Ware made from layers of clays of different colour. Mainly Staffordshire eighteenth century.

Ageing. Allowing prepared plastic clay to stand for some days or weeks before use. The process is beneficial in that the water becomes evenly distributed.

Albite. A form of felspar containing more sodium oxide than potassium oxide.

Alkali. Some 'basic' substances are known as alkalies, but not all the bases are alkaline. The alkalies – soda, potash and lime – are important fluxes in glazes.

Alkaline glazes, 63, 65

Alumina. Al_2O_3. Oxide of the metal aluminium. Essential ingredient of bodies and glazes, provided by clays and felspars. Deposits of the pure alumina ore – bauxite – are rare. *In clay, 35, 118–19; in rocks, 39–40; percentage in typical ceramic substances, 40; as a refractory, 59; in glazes, 120, 125*

Anorthite. Uncommon form of felspar containing more lime than soda or potash.

Antimony oxide. A poisonous oxide producing yellows in lead glazes.

Ashes, *in glazes, 64; preparation of, 121–2; analysis of, 125*

Aspdin, Joseph, *52*

Astbury, *65*

Atoms, *combination of, 33; construction of, 33–5*

Aventurine. A form of glaze in which the growth of coloured crystals is encouraged.

B

Babylon, *glaze records, 63; Plate 1*

Baffle walls, *57*

Bag wall. A wall inside the chamber of a down-draught kiln so placed that it directs the flames towards the roof. *See also* baffle walls.

Ball clay. Highly plastic secondary clay which is white or cream when fired. *Origin of, 73; analysis of, 119*

Ball mill. Rotating grinding mill partly filled with pebbles or porcelain balls. Of use only on substances which have already been finely crushed.

Bank kiln. Kiln consisting of either a single long chamber or a series of smaller ones built up a steep hillside. The incline creates sufficient draught without a chimney.

Barium. A rare metal of which the oxide, BaO, is sometimes used as a flux in glazes. Barytes is the name of the common ore (sulphate, $BaSO_4$) and baryta is the name given to the oxide. *Oxide in glazes, 120, 125; carbonate, 124*

Basalt, *formation of, 40–1; in glazes, 122; analysis of, 125*

Basalt ware. Stoneware made from a fine blackened clay body which, when fired, resembles the polished rock. Introduced by Wedgwood in 1768.

Bascom, Willard, *41*

Basic oxides. Most metallic oxides are 'basic' in characteristic. *See* **Acid**.

Bat. Either a kiln shelf or a flat piece of clay such as might be pressed over a mould.

Bat wash. Mixture of infusible substances such as china clay and flint (50/50) painted on kiln shelves to prevent pots sticking during firing.

Technical terms related to industrial work are given full coverage in the *Dictionary of Ceramics* by A. E. Dodd (Information Officer, British Ceramic Research Association). Newnes, 1964.

H

I

J

K

Mullite. A substance formed from clay after heating above 1100° C. $3Al_2O_3.2SiO_2$.

N

Near East, *brickmaking, 51; kilns, 55–6; geology of, 63; quality of wares, 64*

Nepheline syenite. Rock composed of nepheline and felspar. Approximate composition: $K_2O.3Na_2O.4Al_2O_3.8SiO_2$.
See page 121; analysis of, 125

New Art Teaching, *definition of, 25; leaders of, 28*

Nickel oxide. Occasionally used as a colorant giving greys and browns. NiO (grey powder) Ni_2O_3 (black powder). *See page 127.*

Nitre. Potassium nitrate, KNO_3.

O

Ochre. Earth rich in hydrated iron oxide.

Olivine, *formula of, 40*

On-glaze decoration. Low-fired (750° C.) coloured glazes applied as decoration to already glazed ware. Often applied by silk screen or lithography. *See also page 110.*

Opacifier. Substance added to a glaze to make it opaque and white. Usually tin oxide, titanium oxide or zirconia.

Opening material. Non-plastic or pre-fired material added in finely ground form to clay in order to reduce shrinkage. Grog, chamotte or sand are used in this way.

Oriental kilns, *57*

Orthoclase. Commonest type of felspar containing a preponderance of potash among the fluxes in its composition. $K_2O.Al_2O_3.6SiO_2$.

Oxidation. Firing carried out with adequate air supply. This is important between 400° C. and 850° C. when carbon compounds are being burned out of clay and for any glazes containing lead. An electric kiln will always oxidize firings, but care has to be taken with coal or gas fired kilns.

Oxides, *in clay, 35; melting points of, 36; common ones, 39; as colorants, 112, 126–7; preparation of, 113*

Oxide ceramics. Wares shaped from reasonably pure oxide powders – usually those with high melting points such as magnesia (2800° C.) – for scientific purposes. *See page 59 and Plate 8.*

Oxygen, *in ceramics, 35; in the Earth, 39*

P

Packing a kiln, *95–6*

Paste. Obsolete word for body, especially porcelain.

Paris white. Whiting.

Pearl ash. Potassium carbonate. K_2CO_3.

Pebble mill. Ball mill using flints as grinding media.

Peeling. Glaze fault known also as flaking or shivering.

Pegmatite. Rock composed of large crystals caused by exceptionally slow cooling. Source of felspar.

Peptize. Another term for deflocculation.

Peridotite, *40–1*

Periodic kiln. Another name for intermittent kiln.

Periodic Table of the Elements, *34–5, 126*

Persia, *import of porcelain, 63; lustrewares, 64*

Petuntse. Chinese name for Cornish stone or China stone.

Pinching, *methods, 106; models, illustrations pages 24 and 25; Plates 27, 34 and 39*

Pinholing. Glaze defect caused by the escape of gaseous matter. Increased firing temperature or additional fluxing material will usually ensure that they are smoothed over.

Pipes, *methods of making, 55*

Pitchers. Faulty biscuit ware which is crushed and used as grog.

Placing sand. Fine clean sand used for supporting unglazed pieces during firing.

Plagioclase. Various mixtures of soda and calcium felspar.

Plasticity of clay, *cause of, 73; in ball clay, 74*

Porcelain. Ware made from a white body composed of felspar, china clay and quartz, and fired to a high temperature so that it becomes translucent. *Evolution of, 63–5, Plate 42; insulators, 60 and Plate 9.*

Portland cement. Hydraulic cement produced by firing a mixture of limestone, chalk and clay. *Typical analysis, 40*

Potassium carbonate, *119*

Potassium oxide or **Potash.** Flux, K_2O. Potash is also sometimes used as a name for potassium carbonate. *Percentage in ceramic substances, 40; in rocks, 40; in early glazes, 63; in clay, 73, 119; in glazes, 120, 124.*

Potsherd or **Sherd.** Broken pottery.

Pottery, *in archaeology, 47; discovery of, 61; history of domestic wares, 61–7*

Powdered clay, *usefulness of, 75*

Pressing. Squeezing shapes such as handles by placing soft clay between two pieces of a plaster mould.

Primary air. Main air supply for burning gas or solid fuels. In gas kilns it is mixed with the fuel through a bunsen ring; in solid fuel kilns the primary air enters under the fire bars and passes *through* the fuel.

Primary clay. Clay still lying on the site of its formation. *See page 73.*

Protons, *34*

Pugmill. A mill through which clay is forced in order to consolidate it. Large versions are often fitted with a vacuum pump so that the clay is extruded ready for use. *See page 78 and Plate 13.*

Pyrites. Iron sulphide, FeS_2. The cause of the familiar brown spots in reduction fired clay.

Pyrometer. A device for measuring temperature, showing also the rise and fall. It is operated by the minute electric current induced when two joined wires of certain rare metals are subjected to heat (a thermocouple). *See page 83.*

Pyrometric cones. Cones of clay and glass mixtures which bend, or begin to melt, at known temperatures. Being ceramic in composition cones also record the work done by the heat, a record of temperature alone being insufficient to show that fusion has taken place. *In use, 83; list of, 129.*

Pyroxene, *formula of, 40*

Q

Quartz. The commonest form of silica. A constituent of all igneous rocks which, on their decay, is carried away as sand. *See page 40; in early glazes, 62; in granite, 72; in glazes, 122.*

Quartzite. Deposits of sand which have been re-formed into hard rock by the cementing action of additional silica in solution.

Queen's Ware. Name given to Wedgwood's cream earthenware by the wife of George III in 1763.

Quenching. Plunging red-hot or molten substances into cold water. With glaze frits this aids subsequent grinding.

R

Raku ware. A type of pottery made originally in Japan from heavily grogged clays coated with soft lead and borax glazes maturing at about 800°C. The cold ware is placed directly into a red-hot kiln and is withdrawn as soon as the glaze appears fused. It may then be plunged into cold water to cool for immediate use. *Description of process, 84; suitable bodies, 75; suitable glazes, 125.*

Ramming or **Tamping.** Compressing clay or concrete into a mould by repeated hammering.

Rational analysis. Analysis of a substance into constituent minerals instead of constituent chemicals. For instance, granite is composed of about 52% felspar, 31% quartz and 12% mica. A chemical analysis of granite would show the total quantity of silica present in all three minerals as well as the other oxides present in felspar and mica (*see page 125*).

Raw glaze. A glaze in which no ingredients have previously been fritted.

Raw glazing. Applying any glaze (not necessarily a 'raw glaze') to damp, unfired claywire. Synonymous with ONCE-FIRED WARE.

Recuperation. The use of the heat from exhaust gases to pre-heat air or gas before they are burned.

Red clay, *analysis of, 40; red clay wares, 63–4; use of, 74–5; composition of, 119; in glazes, 120, 127*

Red lead. Lead oxide, Pb_3O_4.

Reduction firing. Firing ware in an atmosphere deprived of oxygen. In a coal fired kiln such an atmosphere occurs each time it is stoked; in a gas kiln it may be achieved by turning the bunsen rings on the burners until the flames are long and flickering. In electric kilns or muffle kilns fired by any fuel it can only be achieved by introducing some form of carbon. Stoneware firings are usually reduced between 1050° C. and 1200° C. and some of the pleasing colour effects associated with ware of this kind are caused by re-oxidation of the firing between 1200° C. and 1280° C. *See also pages 97, 121, 127 and the frontispiece.*

Refractory. A material able to withstand high temperature. *See pages 59–61; Plates 3 and 8.*

Refractory clays, *in kilns, 59; for raku saggars, 85*

Refractory concrete. Aluminous cement (such as Ciment Fondu) mixed with an aggregate of crushed refractory material. *See page 88.*

Relief decoration, *Plates 16, 20, 30 and 31*

Resist. Wax or some other substance used to resist glaze or colouring oxides in decoration. Often used between two glazes of contrasting colour or texture. The wax burns away in the firing.

Rock formation, *39–40*

Rockingham ware. Red clay ware with a dark brown manganese glaze.

Romans, *vaulting methods, illustration page 50; building methods, 50–1; water supplies, 54; kilns, illustration page 56; use of coal, 60; glass, 63; tile, 111*

Rouge Flambé. A red colour produced originally in China by the reduction of copper oxide in a porcelain glaze.

Rutile. Crude ore of titanium oxide containing also some iron oxide. Readily forms crystals in glazes.

S

Saggar. A fireclay box in which ware is packed in solid fuel kilns. Clean fuels – gas and electricity – have made them unnecessary. *Heat absorption of, 58; for raku, 85.*

Salt glaze. A method of glazing in which salt is thrown onto the fire when the kiln temperature is about 1200° C. The sodium in the salt forms a glass with the alumina and silica of the clay. Used commercially only for sewer pipes, but its attractive texture appeals to craftsmen potters. *On sewer pipes, 54–5; history of, 65–6; method, 121; frontispiece.*

Sand. Finely ground quartz. White sands are almost pure silica and are used as a source of this oxide in the glass industry. *Formation of, 72; in clay, 73; as basis of glass, 120.*

Screen. Similar to lawn though used to describe a piece of apparatus for grading particle sizes rather than the mere separation of coarse from fine.

Scythian model, *illustration page 103*

Secondary air. Air passing *over* the fuel to complete combustion, rather than through the fuel as does the primary air. In a gas kiln it is usually pre-heated and admitted into the flame passages.

Secondary clay. All clay that has been naturally transported from its site of formation. On the journey most clays acquire plasticity caused by grinding of the particles as well as additions of other substances such as iron oxide. *See page 73.*

Tin-enamelled ware or **Tin-glaze.** Ware glazed with a mixture opacified with tin oxide. Also known as Delft, Maiolica and faience.

Tin oxide. Common opacifier used in proportions usually of about *10%*. SnO_2. Reacts with Chrome to form an unpleasant pink. *See glazes, 64–5, 127; Plate 40 and frontispiece*

Titanium oxide or **Titania.** Opacifier with a tendency to cause mattness or crystallization. TiO_2. RUTILE is a crude form.

Trailing. A method of applying slip decoration through some form of forcing bag with a fine nozzle.

Tunnel kiln. A kiln, often two to three hundred yards in length, with a permanently heated central zone through which ware passes continuously on refractory lined trucks. *See page 58.*

Turning. Finishing the bottoms of pots made on the wheel. It is necessary to leave some thickness of clay at the bottom of a thrown pot otherwise it would be difficult to lift off the wheel whilst it is still soft. When the pot has dried to leather hardness it is replaced on the wheel upside down and a foot is cut with a steel tool, using the wheel as a lathe.

U

Ultimate Analysis. Analysis in terms of oxides present. See also **Rational Analysis.**

Umber. Naturally occurring hydrated iron oxide.

Under-glaze decoration. Decoration applied to ware before glazing. It becomes part of the glaze, but because of the comparatively high temperature at which it must be fired the range of colour is limited.

Underglaze medium. Thin gum to be used with oxides or underglaze colours to prevent smudging. Has to be fired away or 'hardened on' before glaze can be applied. On-glaze medium is oily to make possible the application of colours over glazed surfaces.

Unglazed wares, *65*

Universe, *geography of, 36–8*

Up-draught kiln. Comparatively inefficient kiln in which the gases pass once through the chamber and leave by a flue in the roof. *See page 57; building of, 83–8*

Ur, *ziggurat, 50; drainage, 54*

Uranium oxide. Colorant giving reds or yellows – when you can get it. U_3O_8

V

Vanadium oxide. Colorant producing yellows when tin oxide or titania is present. V_2O_5. *See page 127.*

Vegetable matter, *in clays, 73–4; in glazes, 121*

Vermiculite. A form of mica which expands rapidly when heated to 900° C. providing a useful heat insulation material.

Vibrating mill. Grinding mill operated by vibration. This type is rapidly replacing the old rotary ball mills.

Vitrification. Fusion of a clay body during firing so that it is no longer porous. The temperature at which this occurs varies for every clay, and the reaction generally takes place slowly over a range of temperature. Above these temperatures distortion and bloating occur.

W

Wad box. *See* **Dod box.**

Water, *in clay, 35, 118*

Water of plasticity, *33*

Water-smoking period. The temperature range between 100° C. and 250° C. when steam is evolved from claywares. Fast firing at this stage will cause ware to shatter into dust.

Weathering. Alternate drying, wetting, freezing and thawing over one or two seasons improves the plasticity of newly dug clay.

Wedging. Removal of air pockets in clay by repeatedly banging a wedge-shaped piece into a flat piece lying on a firm bench. The wedge represents half the total piece of clay, and the cutting is done in a different plane each time so that the clay is evenly treated. *See pages 77–8.*

Wedgwood, *61; whiteware, 65–6*

Wheels, *62, 66; in schools, 110*

Whirler. Hand operated wheel for decorating.

White lead. Lead carbonate. $2PbCO_3.Pb(OH)_2$.

Whiting. Practically pure calcium carbonate, $CaCO_3$. *In glazes, 122 and 124.*

Wicket. Temporary wall built to close the entrance to a kiln chamber during firing.

Witherite. Mineral name for barium carbonate, $BaCO_3$.

Z

Ziggurats, *50, illustration page 46*

Zinc oxide. Flux and opacifier which has also a marked effect on certain colours. ZnO. *In glaze, 120*

Zircon. Naturally occurring combination of zirconia and silica, ZrO_2SiO_2. Used as a refractory material and as an opacifier.

Zirconia. Zirconium oxide, ZrO_2. Refractory material.